SRA

REAL SCIENCE

William C. Kyle, Jr.   **Joseph H. Rubinstein**   **Carolyn J. Vega**

A Division of The McGraw·Hill Companies

Columbus, Ohio

Authors

William C. Kyle, Jr.
E. Desmond Lee Family
   Professor of Science Education
University of Missouri – St. Louis
St. Louis, Missouri

Joseph H. Rubinstein
Professor of Education
Coker College
Hartsville, South Carolina

Carolyn J. Vega
Classroom Teacher
Nye Elementary
San Diego Unified School District
San Diego, California

PHOTO CREDITS
Cover Photo: © Gerben Oppermans/Tony Stone Images

SRA/McGraw-Hill

A Division of The McGraw-Hill Companies

Send all inquiries to:
SRA/McGraw-Hill
8787 Orion Place
Columbus, OH 43240-4027

Printed in the United States of America.

ISBN 0-02-6838028

2 3 4 5 6 7 8 9 RRW 05 04 03 02 01 00

Content Consultants

Gordon J. Aubrecht II
Professor of Physics
The Ohio State University
at Marion
Marion, Ohio

William I. Ausich
Professor of Geological
Sciences
The Ohio State University
Columbus, Ohio

**Linda A. Berne, Ed.D.,
CHES**
Professor/Health Promotion
The University of
North Carolina
Charlotte, North Carolina

Robert Burnham
Science Writer
Hales Corners, Wisconsin

Dr. Thomas A. Davies
Texas A&M University
College Station, Texas

Nerma Coats Henderson
Science Teacher
Pickerington Local
School District
Pickerington, Ohio

Dr. Tom Murphree
Naval Postgraduate School
Monterey, California

Harold Pratt
President, Educational
Consultants, Inc.
Littleton, Colorado

Mary Jane Roscoe
Teacher/Gifted And
Talented Program
Columbus, Ohio

Mark A. Seals
Assistant Professor
Alma College
Alma, Michigan

Sidney E. White
Professor Emeritus
of Geology
The Ohio State University
Columbus, Ohio

Ranae M. Wooley
Molecular Biologist
Riverside, California

Reviewers

Stacey M. Benson
Teacher
Clarksville Montgomery
County Schools
Clarksville, Tennessee

Mary Coppage
Teacher
Garden Grove Elementary
Winter Haven, Florida

Linda Cramer
Teacher
Huber Ridge Elementary
Westerville, Ohio

John Dodson
Teacher
West Clayton
Elementary School
Clayton, North Carolina

Cathy A. Flannery
Science Department
Chairperson/Biology
Instructor
LaSalle-Peru Township
High School
LaSalle, Illinois

Cynthia Gardner
Exceptional Children's
Teacher
Balls Creek Elementary
Conover, North Carolina

Laurie Gipson
Teacher
West Clayton
Elementary School
Clayton, North Carolina

Judythe M. Hazel
Principal and Science
Specialist
Evans Elementary
Tempe, Arizona

Melissa E. Hogan
Teacher
Milwaukee Spanish
Immersion School
Milwaukee, Wisconsin

David Kotkosky
Teacher
Fries Avenue School
Los Angeles, California

Sheryl Kurtin
Curriculum Coordinator, K-5
Sarasota County
School Board
Sarasota, Florida

Michelle Maresh
Teacher
Yucca Valley
Elementary School
Yucca Valley, California

Sherry V. Reynolds, Ed.D.
Teacher
Stillwater Public
School System
Stillwater, Oklahoma

Carol J. Skousen
Teacher
Twin Peaks Elementary
Salt Lake City, Utah

M. Kate Thiry
Teacher
Wright Elementary
Dublin, Ohio

Life Science

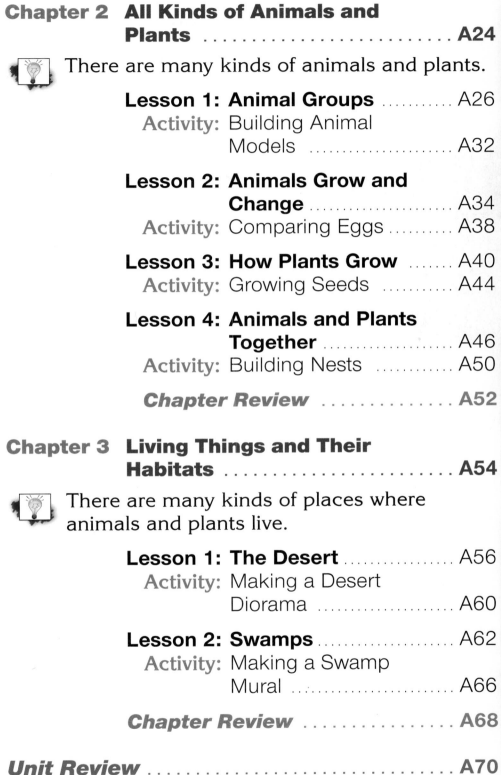

UNIT

B

Earth Science

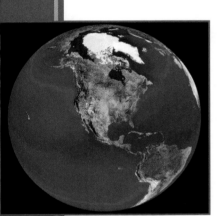

UNIT C

Physical Science

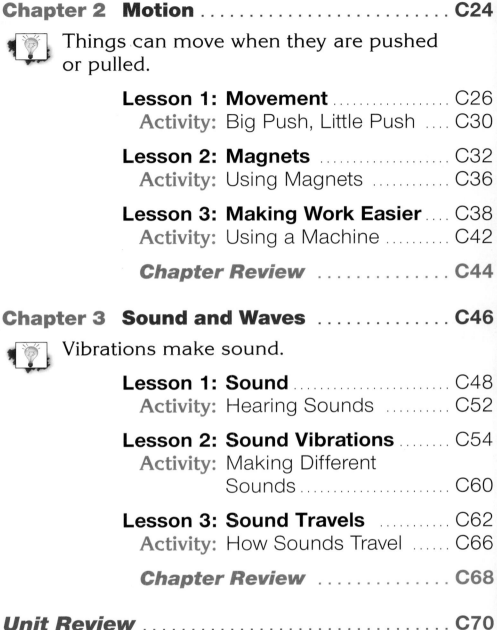

UNIT D

Health Science

Science Process Skills

Scientists use process skills in their work. These skills help them to study science. Process skills also help them to discover new things.

Process skills will help you to discover more about science. You will use these skills in your science activities. Read about each skill. Think about how you already use some of these skills every day. Did you have any idea that you were such a scientist?

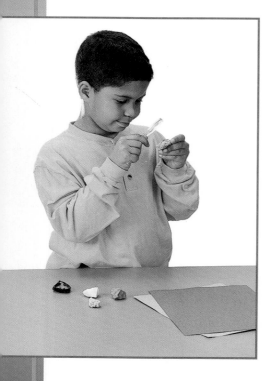

OBSERVING

Find out about objects and events using your senses. You observe by seeing, hearing, touching, tasting, and smelling.

Looking at a rock with a hand lens is observing.

COMMUNICATING

Tell others what you know by speaking, writing, drawing, or using body language.

Drawing a picture of a frog is a way of communicating in science.

CLASSIFYING

Sort objects and events into groups. The sorted objects should all be alike in some way.

Sorting crayons by their colors is a way of classifying.

USING NUMBERS

Use math skills to help understand and study science.

Counting the number of rainy days in a month is using numbers.

MEASURING

Use measures of time, distance, length, size, weight, volume, mass, and temperature to compare objects or events. Measuring also includes using standard measurement tools to find answers.

Measuring skills include **using a stopwatch** to find out how many seconds it takes two worms to travel a distance of 20 cm.

CONSTRUCTING MODELS

Draw pictures or build models to help tell about thoughts or ideas or to show how things happen.

Constructing models of spiders and insects helps you learn about them.

INFERRING

Use what you observe to help explain why something happened or will happen.

You could **infer** that it is summer because the swimming pool is crowded with children.

PREDICTING

Tell what you expect to happen in the future. Predictions are based on earlier observations.

You know that juice bars can melt. You could **predict** that a juice bar will melt if left in the sun.

INTERPRETING DATA

See patterns or explain the meaning of information that you collect.

You are interpreting data when you **record** the temperature for one week and **answer** questions about whether it is hot or cold outside.

IDENTIFYING AND CONTROLLING VARIABLES

Change one thing to see how it affects what happens.

You can **control** the amount of light plant leaves get. Covering some of the leaves on a plant with foil allows you to observe how plant leaves react to light.

HYPOTHESIZING

Tell how or why something happens. Test the hypothesis to see if it is true or false.

You can **say** plants need water to grow. You have to **test** it with an experiment before you can say it is true.

Defining Operationally

Tell what something is by describing what you observe or what something does.

Saying soil is something plants grow in is a way to define soil operationally.

Designing Investigations

Plan investigations to gather data that will support or not support a hypothesis. The design of the investigation determines which variable will be changed, how it will be changed, and what type of data is expected.

You can **design an investigation** to test how sunlight affects plants. Place one plant in the sunlight and an identical plant in a closet. This will allow you to control the variable of sunlight.

Experimenting

Do an investigation to get information about objects, events, and things around you.

Experimenting pulls together all of the other process skills.

UNIT A

Life Science

Animal and Plant Needs

Animals and plants are living things. They need food, water, and air to grow.

Flowers, grass, dogs, and starfish are living things. What living things are in this picture? What things are not living?

The Big IDEA

Animals and plants have needs.

CHAPTER SCIENCE INVESTIGATION

See how animals and plants live together. Find out what to do in your *Activity Journal.*

Animals

Let's Find Out

- What animals need to live
- What body parts animals use to eat

Words to Know

food

water

air

teeth

beaks

The Big QUESTION

How can you tell what an animal eats?

Animal Needs

Animals have needs. They need **food, water,** and **air.** Animals also need places where they can live. What do animals need these things for?

People are animals. People need these things, too.

Animals need food. Some animals eat plants. Some animals eat other animals.

Plant eater

Meat eater

Eating Food

Cow

Lion

Some animals have **teeth.** Teeth can have different shapes. They can be flat or pointed. Flat teeth are good for chewing plants. Animals with pointed teeth can chew meat.

People have both kinds of teeth—some are flat and some are pointed. People can eat plants *and* meat.

A6

Birds have no teeth. They have **beaks** to help them eat. Some birds have small, thick beaks. These birds eat seeds.

Some birds have sharp, hooked beaks. These birds eat animals.

Cardinal

Bald Eagle

Look at this bird's beak. What do you think this bird eats?

CHECKPOINT

1. What do animals need to live?

2. What body parts do animals use to eat?

 How can you tell what an animal eats?

ACTIVITY
Building a Beak

Find Out

Do this activity to see how beaks help birds get food.

Process Skills

Constructing
Models
Predicting
Observing
Communicating

WHAT YOU NEED

nuts

paper plates

birdseed

tweezers

yarn

clothespin

teaspoons

tongs   Activity Journal

WHAT TO DO

1. Put birdseed on one plate. Put nuts on another plate. Put a piece of yarn on the third plate.

2. Imagine that each of the tools is a bird's beak. **Predict** what each beak will pick up.

3. Use each beak to try to pick up the birdseed. **Write** what happened.

4. Use each beak to try to pick up the nuts. **Write** what happened.

5. Use each beak to try to pick up the yarn. **Write** what happened.

WHAT HAPPENED

1. How are the tools like beaks?
2. What did each tool pick up best?

WHAT IF

Look at the beaks of birds near your school or home. From the shape of their beaks, tell what they can eat.

Plants

Let's Find Out
- What the parts of a plant are
- Where seeds are made

Words to Know

roots
leaves
stems
flowers
seeds

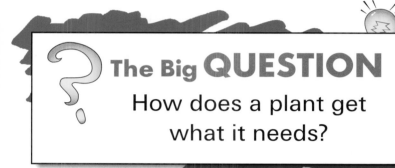

The Big QUESTION

How does a plant get what it needs?

Plant Parts

Plants are living things. They have needs just like animals. Plants need food, water, and air. Plants need sunlight too.

Plants have parts. Plants have **roots.** Most have **leaves** and **stems.** Many plants have **flowers.** These parts help plants get what they need.

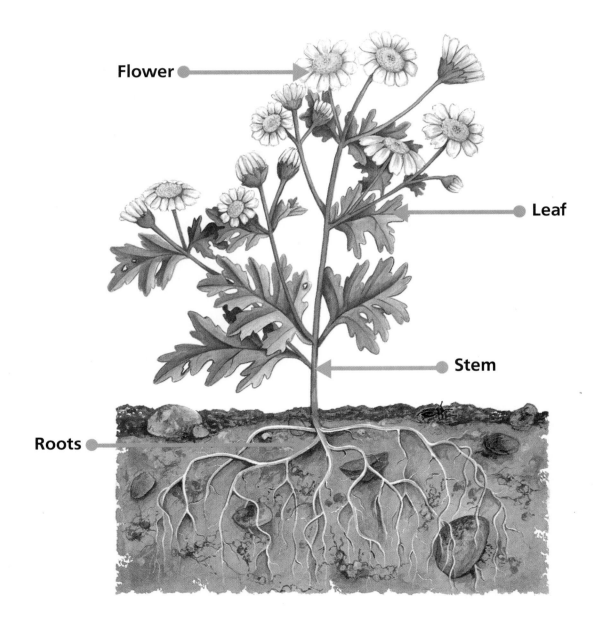

Flower

Leaf

Stem

Roots

What Plant Parts Do

Roots take in water and nutrients from soil. Roots hold plants in the ground.

Green leaves help plants make food. They need sunlight to do this. Plants use the food to grow.

Sunflower

Sunflower seeds

Stems carry water and nutrients from the roots to the leaves.

Many plants grow flowers. Flowers can be many different colors.

Seeds are made in flowers. They can grow into new plants.

CHECKPOINT

1. What are the parts of a plant?

2. Where are seeds made?

 How does a plant get what it needs?

ACTIVITY
How Plants Get Water

WHAT YOU NEED

Find Out

Do this activity to see how plants get water.

Process Skills

Observing
Communicating
Inferring
Predicting

stalk of celery with leaves

jar

water

red food coloring

Activity Journal

WHAT TO DO

1. Fill the jar with water.
2. Place the celery in the jar.
3. Add a few drops of food coloring. Stir.

4. **Observe** the celery.

5. **Draw** what you see.

WHAT HAPPENED

1. What happened to the celery?

2. How do you know that water moved through the stem?

WHAT IF

What would happen if you used a different kind of plant?

Habitats

Let's Find Out
- What animals and plants live in a meadow
- What animals and plants live in an ocean

Words to Know
meadow
habitat
ocean

The Big QUESTION
What do animals and plants have in their habitats?

Meadow

Look at this picture. This is a **meadow.** Bees, flowers, and other living things live and grow here. This is their **habitat.** Animals and plants have what they need in their habitats.

These animals have what they need in a meadow. They find the food they eat there. What do you think these animals eat?

Ocean

Look at this picture. This is an **ocean.** Fish, coral, and other living things live and grow here. This is their habitat.

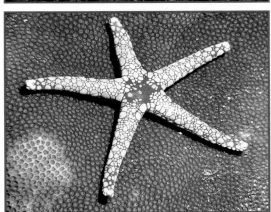

These animals have what they need in an ocean. They find the food they eat there. What do you think these animals eat?

CHECKPOINT

1. What animals and plants live in a meadow?

2. What animals and plants live in an ocean?

 What do animals and plants have in their habitats?

ACTIVITY
Naming Habitats

Find Out
Do this activity to see how animals use plants.

Process Skills
Observing
Communicating

WHAT YOU NEED

paper

magazines

scissors

Activity Journal

WHAT TO DO

1. **Look** for pictures of animals and plants together.

2. Cut the pictures out. Glue them on your paper.

Safety! **Be careful with scissors.**

3. **Write** the name of the habitat each picture shows.

WHAT HAPPENED

1. **Tell** what habitats you found.

2. What animals and plants did you find together?

WHAT IF

People live in habitats. **Tell** what people have in their habitats.

Review

What I Know

Choose the best word for each sentence.

beaks	seeds	leaves
water	flowers	meadow
ocean	teeth	air
habitat	food	roots
stems		

1. Living things need food, air, and _____.

2. Animals with pointed _____ eat other animals.

3. Birds have _____ to help them eat.

4. _____ help a plant get water from the ground.

5. Green _____ help plants make food.

6. _____ can grow into new plants.

7. A place where animals and plants live is called a _____.

Using What I Know

1. What living things can you find in this picture?

2. What body parts do the animals use to get food?

3. What do animals and plants get in their habitats?

For My *Portfolio*

Think of a place where animals and plants live. Draw some animals and plants that live there.

All Kinds of Animals and Plants

Animals are alike in many ways. Some animals have the same kinds of body parts. Some animals move in the same way.
How are these animals alike?

The Big IDEA

There are many kinds of animals and plants.

CHAPTER **SCIENCE INVESTIGATION**

See what living things live near your school. Find out what to do in your *Activity Journal.*

Animal Groups

Let's Find Out

- What mammals and birds are like
- What fish and reptiles are like
- What amphibians and insects are like

Words to Know

mammals
fur
birds
feathers
fish
scales
reptiles
amphibians
insects

The Big QUESTION

What are some groups of animals?

Mammals and Birds

Mammals are a group of animals. Mammals have hair on their skin. This is their body covering. Thick hair is called **fur.**

Most mammals live on land. Some can live in water.

Manatee

Monkey

Birds are a group of animals too. They have **feathers.** Some feathers help birds fly. Some feathers help keep birds warm.

Many birds fly. Some birds cannot fly. Ostriches cannot fly. They walk or run.

Egret

Ostrich

Flight feather

Body feather

Fish and Reptiles

Fish are animals that live in the water. Most fish have **scales** on their bodies. Scales protect fish. All fish have gills. Gills help fish breathe in water. Fish have fins and a tail. Tails help fish move.

Turtle

Snake

Reptiles are another group of animals. Reptiles have scales. Scales protect them. Turtles, snakes, and lizards are reptiles.

Many reptiles have four feet and a tail. They walk or crawl. Snakes do not move like this. Snakes slide on the ground.

Lizard

Amphibians and Insects

Toad

Some animals live on land and in water. These animals are **amphibians.** Frogs, toads, and salamanders are amphibians.

Most amphibians have wet, smooth skin. Many live near water.

Salamander

Ladybug

Butterfly

Katydid

Insects are another group of animals. Insects have six legs. Many insects have wings. Wings help them fly.

Some insects have a hard body covering. This protects their bodies.

Flies and butterflies are insects. Ladybugs and katydids are, too.

Fly

CHECKPOINT

1. What kinds of body coverings do mammals and birds have?

2. How can fish and reptiles move?

3. What kinds of body coverings do amphibians and insects have?

? What are some groups of animals?

A31

ACTIVITY

Building Animal Models

Find Out

Do this activity to make your own animal.

Process Skills

Constructing Models
Observing
Classifying

WHAT YOU NEED

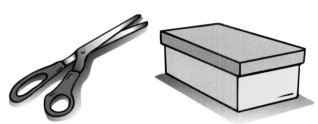

scissors   plastic containers or boxes   glue

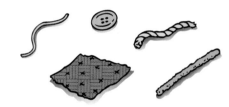

Activity Journal   craft materials

WHAT TO DO

1. Think of an animal. It can be real or pretend.
2. Think about how it looks, how it moves, and what it eats.
3. Use the materials to make your animal.

WHAT HAPPENED

1. What animal did you make?

2. **Look** at your animal. **Look** at the animals other students made. How are the animals the same? How are they different?

WHAT IF

If your animal were real, what kind of habitat would it live in? Why?

Animals Grow and Change

Let's Find Out

- How mammals grow
- How frogs change

Words to Know

eggs
tadpoles

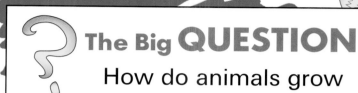

The Big QUESTION

How do animals grow and change?

How Animals Grow

Animals grow and change in different ways. Most young mammals grow inside their mothers. They are born when they are ready.

Young mammals cannot take care of themselves. They need to be fed. They feed on milk from their mothers.

Birds lay **eggs.** A young bird grows inside an egg. Bird eggs have hard shells. The shell keeps the young bird safe inside.

When the young bird is ready, it hatches from the egg.

The young bird cannot fly. It needs to grow feathers. Parent birds take care of it.

How Animals Change

Most fish lay eggs. The covering of fish eggs is not hard like bird eggshells. Fish eggs are soft.

Young fish can swim. They can find their own food.

Most reptiles lay soft eggs. Young reptiles can take care of themselves.

Many young animals look like their parents. Some do not.

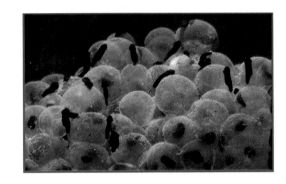

When frogs are born, they are called **tadpoles.** Tadpoles have tails and live in water.

As they get bigger, they lose their tails and can live on land. Then they are called frogs.

CHECKPOINT

1. How do mammals grow?

2. How do frogs change?

? How do animals grow and change?

This insect will change. What will it become?

A37

ACTIVITY

Comparing Eggs

Find Out

Do this activity to see why fish lay eggs in water.

Process Skills

Constructing Models
Predicting
Inferring

WHAT YOU NEED

plate

bowl of water

cooked tapioca

spoon

Activity Journal

WHAT TO DO

1. Put three spoonfuls of tapioca on the plate.

2. Put three spoonfuls of tapioca in the bowl of water. Let both sit.

3. **Predict** how they will feel.

4. **Feel** both.

5. **Tell** what happened.

WHAT HAPPENED

1. Does the dry tapioca feel the same as or different from the wet tapioca?

2. Why do fish lay eggs in water?

WHAT IF

If you used a hard-boiled egg, how would it feel in the water? How would it feel out of the water?

How Plants Grow

Let's Find Out
- What seeds need to grow
- Where seeds come from

Words to Know
fruits
cones

The Big QUESTION

How do different plants make seeds?

Seeds

Many kinds of plants grow from seeds. There are many kinds of seeds. They are different colors, shapes, and sizes.

Each seed has a tiny plant inside. The seed also has some food.

The plant uses the food when it begins to grow. These pictures tell what seeds need to grow.

The seed is planted in the soil. When rain falls, the seed soaks up water.

Tiny roots grow down. A tiny shoot grows up.

The plant gets food from the soil.

The plant needs light from the sun to grow.

Flowers and Cones

Some plants have flowers. A flower is the plant part where a fruit forms.

Fruits have seeds.

Some plants do not have flowers. Their seeds form inside **cones.** Pine trees and fir trees have cones.

CHECKPOINT

1. What do seeds need to grow?

2. Where do seeds come from?

 How do different plants make seeds?

ACTIVITY

Growing Seeds

Find Out

Do this activity to see how seeds grow.

Process Skills

Observing
Predicting
Measuring
Communicating

WHAT YOU NEED

2 cups

paper strips

scoop

clear tape

soil

seeds

water

Activity Journal

WHAT TO DO

1. Tape two seeds to the inside of two cups.
2. Fill the cups with soil.

A44

3. Add water to the soil.

4. Put the cups in a warm, sunny place.

5. **Measure** your plants as they grow. Use the paper strips.

6. Repeat Steps 1–5.

WHAT HAPPENED

1. How tall did your plants grow?

2. Did your plants grow the same each time?

WHAT IF

What would happen if you planted a different kind of seed?

Animals and Plants Together

Let's Find Out
- How animals use plants
- How animals help plants

Words to Know
nests
pollen

 The Big QUESTION
How do animals and plants help each other?

Animals Need Plants

Animals and plants can live in the same places. Animals and plants need each other.

Some animals get their food from plants. Can you name an animal that eats plants?

Some animals make their homes from plants. Some animals use trees for homes. Birds use twigs, branches, and leaves to build **nests.** What other animals live in trees?

Weaverbirds' nests

Elf owl in cactus

Cliff swallows' nests

Grebe's nest

Plants Need Animals

Some plants need animals to spread their seeds. Animals can carry seeds. Seeds stick to an animal's fur. Some seeds stick to feathers. Animals carry seeds to new places. The seeds fall and can grow into new plants.

Flowers have **pollen.** Flowers need pollen to make seeds.

Some animals carry pollen to other flowers. Bees and hummingbirds carry pollen.

Pollen

Bee

Hummingbird

CHECKPOINT

1. How do animals use plants?

2. How do animals help plants?

 How do animals and plants help each other?

A49

ACTIVITY

Building Nests

Find Out

Do this activity to see how birds build their nests.

Process Skills

Constructing Models
Communicating
Observing

WHAT YOU NEED

Activity Journal

paper strips

twigs, branches, and grass

yarn

WHAT TO DO

1. Think about a bird's nest. What is it made of?

2. Use the materials you have to make a nest.

3. **Tell** about your nest.

WHAT HAPPENED

1. **Look** at the other nests in the classroom. How are they alike? How are they different?

2. How is building your nest like a bird building its nest?

WHAT IF

What is another way you could make a home for a bird?

CHAPTER 2

Review

What I Know

Choose the best word for each sentence.

scales	tadpoles	fur
mammals	feathers	reptiles
amphibians	insects	eggs
fruits	cones	nests
pollen	fish	birds

1. Thick hair is called _____.

2. _____ help birds fly.

3. Most fish have _____ on their bodies.

4. Young birds grow inside _____ until they hatch.

5. _____ grow legs and turn into frogs.

6. Seeds come from fruits and _____.

7. Flowers need _____ to make seeds.

Using What I Know

1. What did this plant look like before it started to grow?

2. How is the flower helping the bird?

3. How is the bird helping the flower?

For My **Portfolio**

Think about a plant you like. Write a poem about it.

LIVING THINGS AND THEIR HABITATS

There are many habitats on Earth. Each habitat has many different kinds of animals and plants. Animals and plants have parts that help them live in their habitats.

This place is a habitat. Penguins find the things they need to live there.

The Big IDEA

There are many kinds of places where animals and plants live.

CHAPTER SCIENCE INVESTIGATION

See where animals and plants live. Find out how in your *Activity Journal.*

The Desert

The Big QUESTION

How can some animals and plants live in a hot desert?

Life in a Desert

A **desert** is a very dry place. Many deserts are also very hot during the day.

At night, deserts can get very cool.

Many animals and plants live in a desert.

Great horned owl

Lizard

Desert animals can keep cool when it is hot. Some desert animals stay in the shade during the day.

At night, when it is cool, they look for food. Owls can see well at night. This owl looks for food at night. Lizards also hunt at night.

Desert Plants

The **cactus** is a desert plant. Many kinds of cactus plants live in a desert. These plants have many roots. They take in water quickly when it rains.

The saguaro cactus is a plant in the desert. It can live a long time. It stores water in its stem. The saguaro cactus does not have leaves. It has spines. Spines protect it from animals in the desert.

CHECKPOINT

1. Why do animals in the desert look for food at night?

2. How do cactus plants get water?

?. How can some animals and plants live in a hot desert?

ACTIVITY

Making a Desert Diorama

Find Out

Do this activity to see what a desert looks like and how animals and plants live there.

Process Skills

**Constructing
Models
Communicating**

WHAT YOU NEED

crayons

scissors

construction paper

shoe box

glue

goggles

sand

small rocks

Activity Journal

WHAT TO DO

1. Think about what a desert is like. Make the inside of your shoe box look like a desert.

2. **Show** what the ground and sky look like.

3. **Draw** and cut out desert animals and plants to go in your desert.

WHAT HAPPENED

1. What did you put in your desert?

2. How can your animals and plants live in a desert?

WHAT IF

Tell how you could change your desert to show night.

Swamps

Let's Find Out

- What a swamp is like
- What plants grow in swamps

Words to Know

swamps
egrets
cattails

 **The Big QUESTION**

Why do some animals and plants live in swamps?

Animals in a Swamp

Swamps are very wet. Many animals live in a swamp. They find what they need there.

Fish live in swamp water. Dragonflies fly above swamps. Many kinds of birds live in swamps.

Egrets are birds that live in swamps. They have long legs. They can stand in swamp water.

Alligators and crocodiles also live in swamps.

American alligator

Swamp Plants

Many plants live in swamps.
Some trees live in the water.

Cattails are swamp plants. Their roots grow in water. Their leaves grow above the water.

CHECKPOINT

1. What is a swamp like?

2. What plants grow in swamps?

? Why do some animals and plants live in swamps?

ACTIVITY
Making a Swamp Mural

Find Out
Do this activity to see what animals and plants live in a swamp.

Process Skills
Constructing
Models
Communicating

WHAT YOU NEED

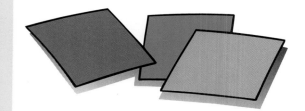
construction paper

glue

scissors

crayons

paper

Activity Journal

WHAT TO DO

1. **Draw** pictures of swamp animals and plants that live in the water.

2. **Draw** pictures of swamp animals and plants that live out of the water.

3. Color the pictures and cut them out.

4. Glue the pictures onto the mural background.

WHAT HAPPENED

1. **Name** some animals in your swamp.

2. **Name** some plants in your swamp.

WHAT IF

What does your mural look like? **Tell** what the animals are doing.

Review

What I Know

Choose the best word for each sentence.

cattails	cactus	swamps
egrets	desert	

1. Many _____ animals look for food at night.

2. The _____ is a desert plant.

3. Alligators live in _____.

4. _____ are swamp birds.

5. _____ are plants that grow in swamps.

Using What I Know

1. Name the animals and plants in each picture.

2. What habitat does each picture show?

3. Is it wet or dry in these habitats?

4. Tell what the animals in the pictures eat.

5. Tell how these habitats change at night.

For My **Portfolio**

Pretend you went to visit a desert or swamp. Write a letter about your trip.

Unit Review

Telling About What I Learned

1. Animals and plants have needs. Tell three things plants and animals need.

2. There are many kinds of animals and plants. Name two of each.

3. Animals and plants live in habitats. Name one animal and where it lives.

Problem Solving

Use the picture to answer the questions.

1. What animals and plants do you see?

2. How do they help each other?

Something to Do

Work in a group. Choose a habitat.
Invent a dance about animals and
plants in your habitat. Move like the
animals and grow like the plants.
When the music changes, change
habitats.

UNIT B

Earth Science

1

Weather

The weather always changes. It can be sunny one day. It can be rainy the next day. What will the weather be tomorrow?

The Big **IDEA**

You can see, feel, and measure weather.

CHAPTER SCIENCE INVESTIGATION

Build a weather station. Watch how the weather changes each day. Find out what to do in your *Activity Journal.*

The Sun and Weather

Let's Find Out

- What the sun warms on Earth
- What the sun can do to puddles

Words to Know

sun

Earth

air

weather

wind

The Big QUESTION

Why is the sun important to weather?

The Sun and Earth

The **sun** warms **Earth.** The sun warms the land, water, and air.

Air is all around us. Air tells us about the **weather.** It can be warm. It can be cool.

Air moves across the land and water. The moving air is **wind.** Sometimes the wind can blow hard.

The Sun Shines

The sun warms the water. The
water goes into the air. The
puddles dry up. It rains. The rain
makes new puddles.

The sun always shines. On cloudy days the sun is still above you. Even at night, the sun shines on the other side of Earth. Day and night, the sun is always there.

CHECKPOINT

1. What does the sun warm on Earth?

2. What can the sun do to puddles?

 Why is the sun important to weather?

ACTIVITY
Warming the Land

Find Out
Do this activity to see how the sun warms land.

Process Skills
Observing
Predicting
Communicating

WHAT YOU NEED

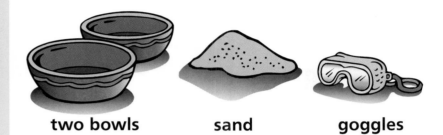

two bowls   **sand**   **goggles**

Activity Journal

clock

WHAT TO DO

1. Fill two bowls with sand. **Touch** the sand in each bowl.

2 Place one bowl in a sunny spot. Place the other bowl in the shade.

3. Wait 30 minutes.

4. **Predict** how the sand in each bowl will feel.

5. **Touch** the sand in each bowl again.

6. **Record** what you **observe.**

WHAT HAPPENED

1. After 30 minutes, which bowl of sand was warmer?

2. Why do you think this happened?

WHAT IF

What would happen if you did this activity on a cloudy day?

Measuring the Weather

Let's Find Out

- How to tell the air temperature
- How we use weather instruments

Words to Know

temperature
thermometer
rain gauge
wind sock
predict

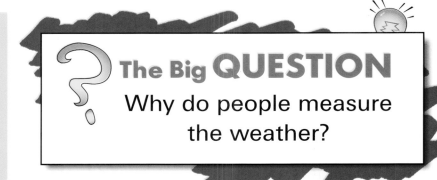

The Big QUESTION

Why do people measure the weather?

Measuring Temperature

Sometimes the air feels warm. Sometimes it feels cold. It can be cold even when the sun is shining.

The **temperature** tells how warm or cool the air is. Air that is warm has a high temperature. Air that is cool has a low temperature.

You can use a **thermometer** to measure the air temperature.

More Weather Instruments

Some days it rains hard. Some days it does not rain at all. You can measure how much it rains with a **rain gauge.** A rain gauge shows in numbers how much rain falls.

Sometimes you see leaves move when the wind blows. Then you can tell which way the wind is blowing.

You can use a **wind sock** to find out which way the wind is blowing.

Weather instruments can measure how weather changes from day to day. Scientists use weather measurements to **predict** the weather. What do you think the weather will be tomorrow?

CHECKPOINT

1. What weather instrument measures air temperature?

2. How do we use weather instruments?

Why do people measure the weather?

ACTIVITY

Reading a Thermometer

Find Out
Do this activity to see how you can measure the air temperature.

Process Skills
Communicating
Observing
Measuring

WHAT YOU NEED

two thermometers

Activity Journal

WHAT TO DO

1. Hang one thermometer outside. Keep another one in the classroom.

2. **Talk** about how the air in the classroom feels.

3. **Look** at the thermometer in the classroom.

4. **Talk** about how the air outside feels.

5. **Look** at the thermometer outside.

6. Repeat the activity to check your readings.

WHAT HAPPENED

1. Which line was longer?

2. Which thermometer was in a warmer place?

WHAT IF

What would happen if you did this activity at a different time of year?

The Seasons

Let's Find Out

- What the four seasons are
- How the weather can change from season to season

Words to Know

season
winter
spring
summer
fall

The Big QUESTION

What happens in each season?

Four Seasons

A **season** is a time of year with its own kind of weather. There are four seasons—winter, spring, summer, and fall. Weather can change from season to season.

Winter days have the least amount of daylight. It may get dark before dinner. Winter is the coldest season. Even in warm places, the weather gets cooler. In some places it snows.

Spring days have more daylight than winter days. The air is warmer too. Many kinds of plants begin to grow and bloom in spring.

Seasons Change

Summer days have the most daylight. It may still be light at bedtime. In summer, the air is warmer than in spring. Summer is the warmest season.

Fall comes after summer. Fall days have fewer hours of sunlight than summer days. The air is cooler too. Leaves fall off some trees.

In some places the weather changes a lot from season to season. In other places you may not see much change. How do the seasons change where you live?

CHECKPOINT

1. What are the four seasons?

2. How is the weather different in each season?

 What happens in each season?

ACTIVITY
Making a Season Wheel

Find Out
Do this activity to see how the seasons change in a year.

Process Skills
Communicating

WHAT YOU NEED

paper plate

pencil

crayons

Activity Journal

WHAT TO DO

1. With your pencil, draw a line down the middle of the paper plate. Draw another line across it to make four equal parts.

2. Write the name of the seasons in order, one in each part.

3. **Draw** yourself the way you would look in each season.

4. **Draw** things that you do in each season.

5. **Tell** about what you drew.

WHAT HAPPENED

1. What did you draw in each season?

2. How are the seasons different where you live?

WHAT IF

What could you do outdoors on the first day of school where you live?

Review

What I Know

Choose the best word for each sentence.

air	weather	Earth
temperature	wind sock	predict
rain gauge	summer	wind
sun	season	winter
thermometer	fall	spring

1. Moving air is called _____.

2. The _____ is always shining.

3. A _____ measures air temperature.

4. A _____ shows how much rain falls.

5. A _____ is a time of year.

6. The coldest season is _____.

7. _____ is the warmest season.

Using What I Know

1. Tell about the weather in the picture.

2. Tell how weather instruments can measure the weather in the picture.

3. What season do you see in the picture?

For My Portfolio

Cut out pictures from old magazines. Make a scrapbook with pictures of each season. Pick your favorite season. Draw a picture of yourself in that season. What clothes are you wearing? What are you doing?

CLiMate

There are many places to live on Earth. Different animals and plants live in each place.

The weather can be different in different places. Some places are warm. Some places are cool. Some places are rainy and some places are dry.

The Big IDEA

Earth has different climates.

CHAPTER SCIENCE INVESTIGATION

Learn what people do in different climates. Find out what to do in your *Activity Journal.*

The Desert

Let's Find Out

- How much it rains in a desert
- How temperature changes in a desert

Words to Know

climate
desert
dry
hot

The Big QUESTION

What is the climate of a desert?

A Very Dry Place

Earth has many climates. The **climate** of a place is what the weather is like most of the time.

The **desert** is a place where animals and plants live. All deserts have a **dry** climate. Deserts get very little rain or snow. It may not rain for months and months. Then it may rain very hard. But the sun and wind dry up much of the water quickly.

Day and Night

During the day, many deserts are very **hot.** The air temperature is very high. The sand in deserts gets hot, too.

When the sun goes down, deserts get cold. The air temperature is low. The sand is cold, too.

Some deserts are cold all the time. Sometimes it snows, but only a little.

CHECKPOINT

1. How much does it rain in a desert?

2. How does the temperature in the desert change from day to night?

 What is the climate of a desert?

ACTIVITY

Hot and Dry

Find Out
Do this activity to see what happens to rain in a desert.

Process Skills
Measuring
Predicting
Observing
Communicating

WHAT YOU NEED

sand

soil

two plates

clock

spoon

water

Activity Journal

WHAT TO DO

1. Put the sand on one plate. Put the soil on the other plate.

2. Pour five spoonfuls of water on the sand. Pour five spoonfuls of water on the soil.

3. Set both plates in a sunny place.

4. Wait 30 minutes. **Predict** how the sand and soil will feel.

5. **Draw** what you **see.**

WHAT HAPPENED

1. What happened to the water on the sand? On the soil?

2. Why do you think this happened?

WHAT IF

What would happen if you put the plates of sand and soil in a dark place?

The Tropical Rain Forest

Let's Find Out

- How much rain falls in a tropical rain forest
- What the temperature is in a tropical rain forest

Words to Know

tropical rain forest
wet
humid

The Big QUESTION

What is the climate of a tropical rain forest?

Rainy Days

The **tropical rain forest** has its own climate. Many different animals and plants live there.

Tropical rain forests have a very **wet** climate. It rains there a lot. Sometimes it rains very hard.

Warm Weather

In the tropical rain forest, the weather does not change much. It is warm all year long. Day and night, the rain forest stays warm. The warm, wet climate is just what many living things need.

In the rain forest, trees grow very tall. Trees lose water through their leaves. The water goes back into the air. This makes the air feel **humid.** Humid air feels wet and sticky.

CHECKPOINT

1. How much rain falls in a tropical rain forest?

2. What is the temperature like in a tropical rain forest?

? What is the climate of a tropical rain forest?

ACTIVITY

Water from Plants

Find Out

Do this activity to see why the rain forest air is wet.

Process Skills

Predicting
Observing
Communicating
Inferring

WHAT YOU NEED

water

clear plastic bag

tape

Activity Journal

small plant in a pot

WHAT TO DO

1. Water the plant.
2. Put the clear, plastic bag over the plant. Use tape to close the bag around the stem.

3. Put the plant in a sunny place. **Predict** what will happen.

4. Wait 2–3 hours.

5. **Tell** about what you **see**.

WHAT HAPPENED

1. What happened to the plastic bag?

2. Why did this happen?

WHAT IF

What would happen if you had several plants inside the bag?

The Arctic

Let's Find Out

- What winter is like in the Arctic
- What summer is like in the Arctic

Words to Know

Arctic
cold
ice

The Big QUESTION

What is the climate of the Arctic?

Cold, Dark Winters

The **Arctic** has its own climate. In winter, the Arctic is a very **cold** place. Most of the water is covered with **ice,** and the land is frozen.

The Arctic winter is dark. The sun does not shine very much. The air temperature gets very cold. The weather is dry, but it snows a little.

Summer in the Arctic

In the Arctic summer, the sun shines almost all day and all night. But the sun does not warm the air much. It is still cool.

Some of the ice and snow melts. Plants grow fast in the summer sun. It does not stay sunny for very many weeks. Soon it is dark and very cold again.

CHECKPOINT

1. What is winter like in the Arctic?

2. What is summer like in the Arctic?

 What is the climate of the Arctic?

ACTIVITY

Freezing Earth

Find Out
Do this activity to see what the earth is like in the Arctic.

Process Skills
Observing
Communicating
Inferring
Predicting

WHAT YOU NEED

pie plate

water

soil

Activity Journal

small rocks

WHAT TO DO

1. Cover the bottom of the pie plate with soil and rocks.

2. Cover the soil and rocks with water.

3. Put the pie plate in the freezer until the water is frozen.

4. **Tell** about what you **see.**

WHAT HAPPENED

1. How did the water and soil change?

2. How are the water, soil and rocks in the pie plate like the Arctic?

WHAT IF

What would happen if you put the pan of frozen soil, rocks, and water in a warm place?

Review

What I Know

Choose the best word for each sentence.

dry	Arctic	hot
climate	cold	desert
tropical rain forest	humid	wet
	ice	

1. The _____ of a place is what the weather is like most of the time.

2. The weather is dry and often _____ in many deserts.

3. It rains a lot in a _____.

4. The tropical rain forest has a warm, _____ climate.

5. _____ air feels wet and sticky.

6. The water is covered with ice in the _____.

7. In winter, the Arctic is very _____.

Using What I Know

1. What climates do you see in these pictures?

2. What is the weather like in each picture?

3. What is the weather like where you live?

For My Portfolio

Cut out the weather map from the local newspaper. Find your area on the map. Tell about the weather where you live.

LAND, WATER, AND RESOURCES

You use many things on Earth. You use land, water, and air every day.

Land and water cover Earth and can be found in many forms.

The Big IDEA

Rocks, soil, and water cover Earth.

SCIENCE INVESTIGATION

See what Earth's soil is like. Find out what to do in your *Activity Journal.*

Land and Water

Let's Find Out

- What different landforms look like
- What different bodies of water are like

Words to Know

landforms
salt water
freshwater

The Big QUESTION

What landforms and water are on Earth?

Land

Land on Earth has different shapes. These land shapes are called **landforms.**

Mountains are tall landforms. They are made of rock.

The land between two mountains is low. It is called a valley.

Mountains

Valley

Some land is not tall at all.
Plains are flat land. They have
thick layers of soil. Tell what
landforms each picture shows.

Plains

Water

Ocean

Most of Earth is covered with water. Oceans are large bodies of water. They are wide and deep. The water in oceans is **salt water.**

Lake

Lakes are smaller than oceans. The water in lakes is usually not salty. The water is usually **freshwater.**

Water can move. It can move in streams. It can move in big, wide rivers. Can you tell what each picture shows?

CHECKPOINT

1. Tell what mountains, valleys, and plains look like.

2. Name some different bodies of water.

 What landforms and water are on Earth?

ACTIVITY

Making a Land and Water Collage

Find Out
Do this activity to group landforms of land and water.

Process Skills
Classifying
Communicating

WHAT YOU NEED

paper

pencil

glue

Activity Journal

magazines

scissors

WHAT TO DO

1. Cut out pictures of land and water from magazines. **Safety!** **Be careful with scissors.**

2. Put the pictures on your paper. **Place** land pictures on one side and water pictures on the other side.

3. **Group** all the land pictures that show the same landform. **Group** all the water pictures that show the same kind of body of water.

4. Glue the pictures onto your paper.

5. **Write** what landforms and bodies of water your pictures show.

WHAT HAPPENED

1. What kinds of land does your collage show?

2. What bodies of water did you find?

WHAT IF

Tell another way you could group the land pictures. **Tell** another way you could group the water pictures.

Rocks and Soil

Let's Find Out

- What rocks and minerals are like
- How people use rocks and minerals
- How rocks change

Words to Know

rocks
minerals
sand
soil

The Big QUESTION

What are rocks and soil, and how are they used?

Rocks and Minerals

Earth has many kinds of **rocks.** They are different shapes and sizes.

Basalt

Marble

Slate

Limestone

Sandstone

Granite

Rocks are made from **minerals.**
Some minerals are shiny. Some
are dull. Some minerals are hard
and some are soft. Minerals can
be different colors.

Pyrite

Amethyst

Calcite

Copper

Chrysocolla

Malachite

Using Rocks and Minerals

Rocks are many sizes. Some rocks are very big. Some rocks fit in your hand. Some rocks are tiny.

People use rocks and minerals in many ways. Tell how rocks and minerals are being used in each of these pictures. Tell other ways you have seen rocks and minerals used.

Stone cottage in Ireland

Amethyst

Marble

Talc

Graphite

Large rocks broken
into smaller rocks

Rocks Break Down

Wind and water break down
rocks. Big rocks break into smaller
rocks. Smaller rocks break into
pebbles. Pebbles break into
smaller pebbles. Smaller pebbles
break into **sand.**

Rocks moved by water

Rocks shaped by water

Sand on the beach

Soil is made from rocks too. Soil also has water and air in it.

Not all soil is alike. Some soils are better than others for growing plants.

CHECKPOINT

1. Tell about different kinds of rocks and minerals.

2. How can people use rocks and minerals?

3. How do rocks change?

 What are rocks and soil, and how are they used?

ACTIVITY
Grouping Rocks

Find Out
Do this activity to see how rocks are alike.

Process Skills
Observing
Classifying
Communicating

WHAT YOU NEED

rocks

three pieces of construction paper

hand lens

Activity Journal

WHAT TO DO

1. Put all the rocks on one piece of paper.

2. Use the hand lens to **look** at the rocks carefully.

3. Move the dark-colored rocks to one piece of paper. Move the light-colored rocks to another piece of paper.

4. Move all the rocks back together. Now try to **group** the rocks in a different way. Ask another student to guess how you grouped the rocks.

WHAT HAPPENED

1. **Tell** how you sorted the rocks.

2. **Tell** some other ways you could group the rocks.

WHAT IF

Tell how you could group rocks with your eyes closed.

• LESSON 3

Earth's Resources

Let's Find Out
- How people use Earth's resources
- What you can recycle

Words to Know
land
water
air
resources
recycle

The Big QUESTION
How do we use and take care of Earth?

Resources

People use Earth in many ways. They live and play on the **land.** They grow plants in the soil and use rocks in many different ways.

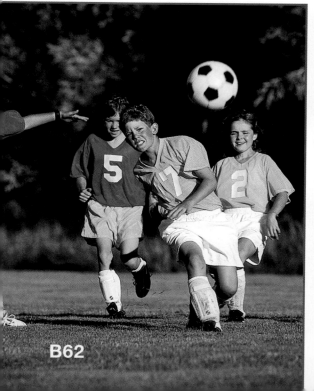

B62

People drink **water** from Earth. They use water for washing and swimming.

People breathe **air** on Earth.

Land, water, and air are **resources.** Resources are the parts of Earth that people use.

Taking Care of Earth

You can help take care of the land, water, and air. Put garbage where it belongs. Don't waste water. Think before you throw things away. Maybe you can reuse them in another way.

Things can be changed so they can be used again. This is how people **recycle.** You can recycle cans, paper, glass, and most plastics.

CHECKPOINT

1. What are some ways people use Earth's resources?

2. What things can you recycle?

 How do we use and take care of Earth?

ACTIVITY

Caring for Earth

Find Out

Do this activity to see how you can recycle Earth's resources.

Process Skills

Observing
Predicting
Communicating

paper you no longer need

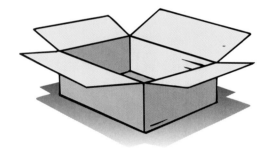

large cardboard box

Activity Journal

WHAT TO DO

1. **Look** at the size of the empty cardboard box. **Look** at the size of the paper you write on in class.

2. **Guess** how much paper your class throws away in a week. **Write** your guess.

3. Every time you finish with a piece of paper, put it in the box instead of throwing it away.

4. **See** how much paper your class uses in one week.

5. When the box is full, you can recycle the paper.

WHAT HAPPENED

1. How much paper did your class collect? Was your guess right?

2. Where would the paper go if you didn't recycle it?

WHAT IF

What other things could you recycle?

Review

What I Know

Choose the best word for each sentence.

minerals	landforms	rocks
water	resources	sand
land	air	soil
recycle	freshwater	salt water

1. Earth's land shapes are called _____.

2. Oceans are full of _____.

3. Rocks are made from _____.

4. Pebbles break into _____.

5. _____ has rocks, water, and air in it.

6. Air, water, and land are Earth's _____.

7. You can _____ cans, paper, and glass so they can be used again.

Using What I Know

1. Tell what landform is in the picture.

2. Tell what body of water is in the picture.

3. Tell what resources you see in the picture.

For My *Portfolio*

Imagine a place that has many landforms. Draw a picture of the place. Label the landforms. Then invent a new landform that you have never seen before. Draw it. What will you call it?

Unit Review

Telling About What I Learned

1. Weather can be observed and measured. Tell what instruments measure weather.

2. Weather patterns are different in different places. Tell about the climate in two places on Earth.

3. Natural resources come from Earth. Name three resources that come from Earth.

Problem Solving

Use the picture to answer the questions.

1. What landforms can you name?

2. What resources can you find?

3. How might this landscape look different in winter?

Something to Do

Build a model of the kinds of landforms and water around you. Use building blocks, clay, rocks, sand, or soil. What landforms did you make?

UNIT C

Physical Science

CHAPTER 1

Forms of Matter

Matter is all around you. Some matter is hard, and some is soft. Some matter is dry, and some is wet. How else can matter be different?

The Big IDEA

Matter can have three forms and can change.

Solids, Liquids, and Gases

Let's Find Out

- What solids are
- What liquids and gases are

Words to Know

matter
solid
liquid
gas

The Big QUESTION

What are three forms of matter?

Solids

Matter is all around you. **Matter** can have three forms. It can be a solid, liquid, or gas.

Some matter is **solid.** A solid has a certain shape.

Some solids have color. Some solids can roll. Some can stack. Some solids float, and some sink.

Tell what these solids can do.

Liquids and Gases

Some matter is **liquid.** Water is a liquid. Liquids pour. Some liquids have color.

How are these liquids different? Do they have a shape?

Some matter is **gas.** You can't see most gases.

Air is a gas. You can't see air.

CHECKPOINT

1. What are solids?

2. What are liquids and gases like?

 What are three forms of matter?

ACTIVITY

Gas Takes Up Space

Find Out
Do this activity to see how a gas takes up space.

Process Skills
Observing
Communicating
Inferring
Predicting

WHAT YOU NEED

Activity Journal

balloon

goggles

WHAT TO DO

1. **Look** at your balloon. **Tell** what it looks like.

2. Blow up the balloon. Tie the end in a knot.

3. **Tell** how the balloon changed.

4. Squeeze the balloon between your hands.

5. **Tell** how it feels.

WHAT HAPPENED

1. How did the balloon change?

2. What shape did the gas take?

WHAT IF

What would happen to the gas in the balloon if you untied the end?

Heat and Matter

Let's Find Out
- How heat moves
- How heat can change water

Words to Know
heat
melt

? **The Big QUESTION**
How can heat change matter?

Heat

Some matter can feel warm. Some matter can feel hot. Some matter can feel cool. And some matter can feel cold.

Heat makes matter feel warmer. What can make you feel warmer?

Heat moves. It moves from warmer things to cooler ones.

Heat makes cold things warmer. We cannot see heat move, but we can feel it. How is heat moving here?

Heat Makes Matter Change

Heat can change matter.

When some things get warmer, they **melt.** Name some things that can melt.

Heat can change water. Tell how water can change if it gets warmer.

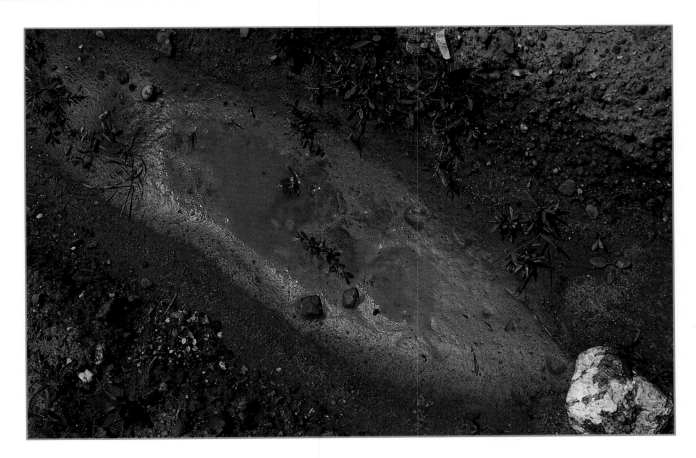

Some things seem to disappear when heat is added. What does heat do to water in puddles?

CHECKPOINT

1. How does heat move?

2. How can heat change water?

 How can heat change matter?

ACTIVITY

Changing Water

Find Out

Do this activity to see how heat changes water.

Process Skills

Observing
Communicating
Inferring
Predicting

WHAT YOU NEED

ice cubes

2 bowls

Activity Journal

WHAT TO DO

1. **Look** at the ice. **Tell** how it looks.

2. Put ice in each bowl.

3. Put the bowls in a warm place. Leave them there for one hour.

4. **Tell** how they look.

5. Repeat Steps 1–4.

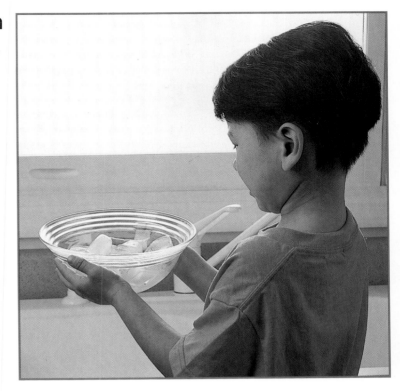

WHAT HAPPENED

1. How did the ice change each time?

2. Did the melted ice look the same each time?

WHAT IF

What would happen if you put the bowls of water into a freezer?

Mixtures

Let's Find Out
- What a mixture is
- How things change when mixed together

Words to Know
mixture

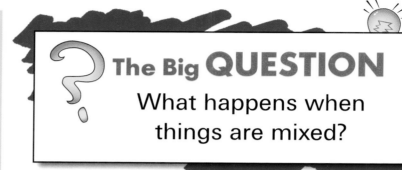

The Big QUESTION
What happens when things are mixed?

Mixing Matter

You can mix things together.

Look at this fruit. What kinds of fruit do you see?

This fruit is a **mixture.**

You see mixtures everyday. A mixture has two or more things in it. What are the mixtures you see here?

Things Change

Some things do not change when mixed. You can mix coins together. The coins do not change. They stay the same.

Some things change when mixed. You can mix cereal and milk. How does the cereal change?

CHECKPOINT

1. What is a mixture?

2. How do things change when mixed together?

? What happens when things are mixed?

ACTIVITY

Making Mixtures

Find Out

Do this activity to see how mixtures can be different.

Process Skills

Observing
Communicating
Predicting

WHAT YOU NEED

canned or cooked peas

water

clear plastic cup

spoon

blender

Activity Journal

WHAT TO DO

1. Put some water in a cup.

2. Put two spoonfuls of peas in the water. Stir.

3. **Draw** what you see.

4. Watch as your teacher pours the mixture into a blender.

5. Put the lid on the blender. Watch as your teacher runs the blender for one minute. **Draw** what you see.

6. Wait one hour. **Predict** what you will **see**.

7. **Draw** what you **see**.

WHAT HAPPENED

1. How are the mixtures alike?

2. What happened to the second mixture after one hour?

WHAT IF

How would this activity be different if you used grapes instead of peas?

Review

What I Know

Choose the best word for each sentence.

solid	melt	liquid
heat	matter	mixture
gas		

1. _____ is all around you.

2. A wood block is a _____.

3. You can pour a _____.

4. Air is a _____.

5. _____ can make matter feel warmer.

6. Butter will _____ if you put it in a warm place.

7. Salad is a _____ of different vegetables.

Using What I Know

1. What solids do you see?

2. What liquids do you see? What gases?

3. How can each one change?

For My Portfolio

Pretend you are a weatherperson. Tell how water can change with the weather.

Motion

Many things can move. Living things can move. How can these animals move? How can you move?

The Big IDEA

Things can move when they are pushed or pulled.

SCIENCE INVESTIGATION

CHAPTER

Make different things move. Find out how in your *Activity Journal.*

Movement

Let's Find Out

- How pushes can be different
- How things can move at different speeds

Words to Know

push
pull
speed

The Big QUESTION

How can you move things?

Pushes and Pulls

You can move things. You can **push.** You can **pull.**

How are these people making things move?

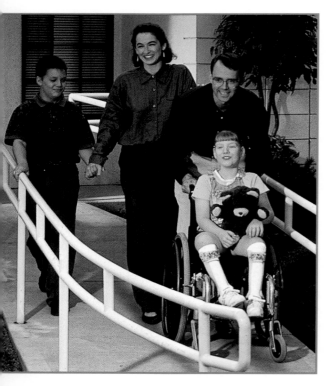

Some things are easy to move. Some are hard to move. Some things need a big push. Some need a little push.

Fast and Slow

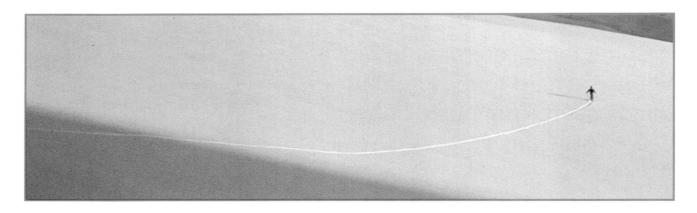

Things can move different ways. Some things move fast. Some move slow.

The **speed** of an object is how fast or slow it goes.

The speed things move can change. Things can move faster. Things can move slower. How can these moving things change speed?

CHECKPOINT

1. How can pushes be different?
2. Name different speeds things can move.
 How can you move things?

ACTIVITY
Big Push, Little Push

Find Out

Do this activity to see how a big push and a little push make an object move.

Process Skills

Predicting
Observing
Measuring
Using Numbers
Communicating

WHAT YOU NEED

paper

wooden blocks

paper clips

Activity Journal

WHAT TO DO

1. Place two blocks next to each other on the edge of the paper.

2. **Predict** which block will go farther.

3. Give one block a little push.

4. Give the other block a big push.

5. Use paper clips to **measure** how far each block moved.

WHAT HAPPENED

1. What was different about the way the blocks moved?

2. Why did the blocks move in different ways?

WHAT IF

What would happen if you pushed the blocks the same way?

Magnets

Let's Find Out
- How magnets can pull
- How magnets can push

Words to Know
magnets
attract
repel

The Big QUESTION
How do magnets move objects?

Magnets Pull

Magnets can move things. Magnets can pull. They can push. What is this magnet doing?

When magnets pull, they **attract.** Magnets attract some metals. Iron is one metal magnets attract.

Magnets Push

Magnets can push, too. When magnets push, they **repel.** Some magnets repel each other. They repel when their ends are alike.

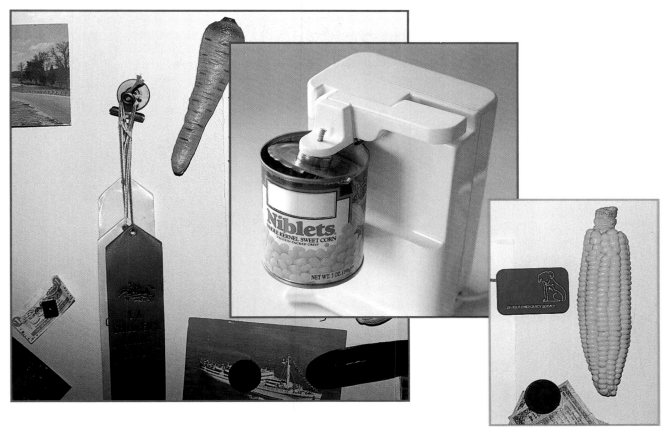

Magnets can be different.
Some are big. Some are small.
Magnets can be different
shapes too.

What magnets do you use?

CHECKPOINT

1. How can magnets pull?

2. How can magnets push?

How do magnets move objects?

ACTIVITY

Using Magnets

Find Out
Do this activity to see how magnets attract.

Process Skills
Predicting
Observing
Classifying
Communicating

WHAT YOU NEED

bowls

paper clip

paper cup

rubber ball

penny

magnet

write-on labels

Activity Journal

WHAT TO DO

1. Place two bowls next to each other. Label one bowl **"Yes."** Label the other bowl **"No."**

2. **Predict** which things the magnet will attract.

3. Hold the magnet close to each object. See which ones the magnet attracts. Try to attract each object. Place each object in the correct bowl.

WHAT HAPPENED

1. **Tell** about the objects in each bowl.

2. What do the objects in the **"Yes"** bowl have in common?

WHAT IF

If you put a sheet of paper between a magnet and an object that the magnet attracts, what would happen?

Making Work Easier

Let's Find Out

- How a ramp makes work easier
- What other machines people use

Words to Know

machines
ramp

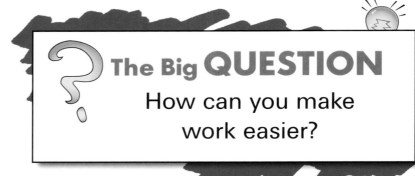

The Big QUESTION

How can you make work easier?

Machines

Light things are easy to move. Some things are heavier. It takes more work to move heavier things.

Machines can make work easier. A **ramp** is a machine. This ramp makes it easier to move things.

People Use Machines

Other machines can make work easier. Tell what these people are using to make work easier.

You use machines every day. You use machines even when you don't know it. Tell what these children are using to make the boat move.

CHECKPOINT

1. How does a ramp make work easier?

2. Name some machines that people use.

 How can you make work easier?

ACTIVITY

Using a Machine

Find Out

Do this activity to see how a machine can make work easier to do.

Process Skills

Observing

Communicating

stack of books

ruler

Activity Journal

WHAT TO DO

1. Try to lift the stack of books with one of your fingers.

2. Now try to lift the books with two fingers.

3. Try to lift the books using your ruler. How did you lift the books?

4. **Watch** your teacher lift the books using the ruler.

WHAT HAPPENED

1. Which was the easiest way to lift the books?

2. **Tell** how using the ruler is like using a machine.

WHAT IF

What are some other tools you could use to lift the stack of books?

Review

What I Know

Choose the best word for each sentence.

magnets	**repel**	**push**
speed	**attract**	**machines**
pull	**ramp**	

1. A _____ or a pull can make something move.

2. A hammer can _____ out a nail.

3. Magnets can repel other _____.

4. A magnet pulls to _____ iron.

5. When magnets push, they _____.

6. _____ make work easier.

7. A _____ is a machine.

Using What I Know

1. Tell how the girl is moving the wagon.

2. How would moving the wagon be different if there were more things in the wagon?

3. Tell another way the girl could move the wagon.

For My Portfolio

Draw some things that magnets can attract. Draw some things that magnets cannot attract.

CHAPTER 3

Sound and Waves

Birds sing.

Dogs bark.

People talk.

Horns blare.

The Big IDEA

Vibrations make sound.

SCIENCE
INVESTIGATION

Listen to different
sounds. Find out
how in your *Activity
Journal.*

Sound

Let's Find Out

- How sounds are different
- What some other kinds of sounds are

Words to Know

loud
soft
music

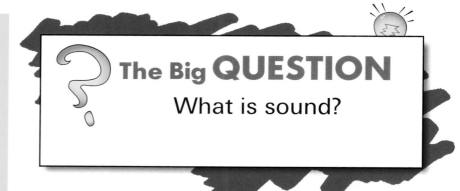

The Big QUESTION
What is sound?

Loud and Soft Sounds

You can make sounds. Clap your hands. Stomp your feet. Whistle. These are sounds.

Some sounds are **loud.** Loud sounds are easy to hear.

Some sounds are **soft.**

Are these sounds loud or soft?

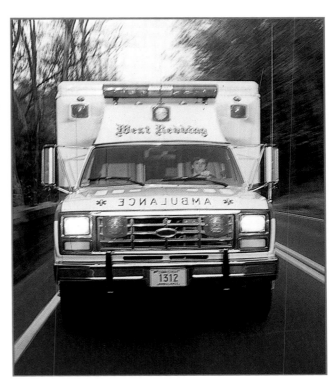

Other Sounds

Some people play instruments.
Instruments make different
sounds. They can play **music.**

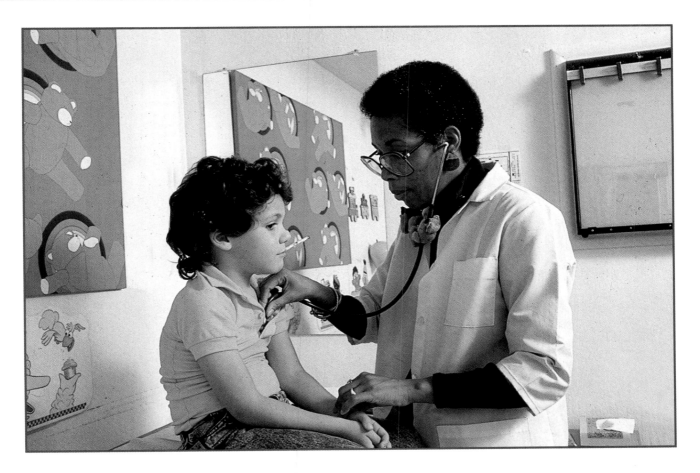

Your heart makes a sound. A doctor can hear it. Do you know what sound your heart makes?

CHECKPOINT

1. How can sounds be different?

2. What are some other sounds?

3. What is sound?

ACTIVITY
Hearing Sounds

Find Out
Do this activity to hear different sounds.

Process Skills
Predicting
Observing
Communicating

WHAT YOU NEED

six metal cans or other containers with tight fitting lids

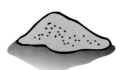

sand

cotton balls

beans

marbles

coins

paper clips

Activity Journal

WHAT TO DO

1. Shake each can. What sound does each one make?

2. **Predict** what is inside each can.

3. **Look** inside each one.

WHAT HAPPENED

1. **Tell** what kinds of sounds you heard.

2. Which things sounded loud? Which made a soft sound?

WHAT IF

How would it sound if water was in the can?

Sound Vibrations

Let's Find Out

- What vibrations are
- What things vibrate to make sounds
- What you need to hear sound

Words to Know

vibrate
vibrations
low
high

The Big QUESTION

What makes sound?

Making Sounds

When things **vibrate,** they move back and forth. These **vibrations** can make sounds.

When a bell vibrates, you hear it ring.

When guitar strings vibrate, you hear music.

Guitar

More Vibrations

Bees buzz. This sound is from their wings. Their wings vibrate.

Frogs croak. What makes this noise?

Your throat vibrates when you talk. Make a **low** sound. Your throat vibrates. Make a **high** sound. Your throat vibrates faster.

Air and Sound

Musical instruments make sounds. Instrument parts vibrate. The strings on a violin vibrate. When the strings vibrate, the air moves. It moves to your ears. Then you hear the sound.

Violin

You need air to hear sound. There is no air in outer space. There are no sounds in outer space.

CHECKPOINT

1. What are vibrations?

2. What are some things that vibrate to make sounds?

3. What do you need to hear sound?

 What makes sound?

ACTIVITY
Making Different Sounds

Find Out
Do this activity to see what makes high and low sounds.

Process Skills
Observing
Communicating
Inferring

WHAT YOU NEED

shoe box

goggles

scissors

three different-sized rubber bands

Activity Journal

WHAT TO DO

1. Carefully cut three slits in each end of the shoe box. **Safety! Be careful with scissors.**

2. Stretch the rubber bands around the box so that they fit in the slots.

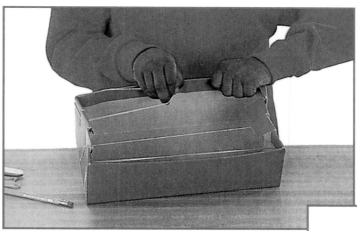

3. Pluck each rubber band. **Listen** to the sound it makes.

WHAT HAPPENED

1. Tell about the sounds the different rubber bands made.

2. Why do you think the sounds were different?

WHAT IF

How could you change the sound that each rubber band made?

Sound Travels

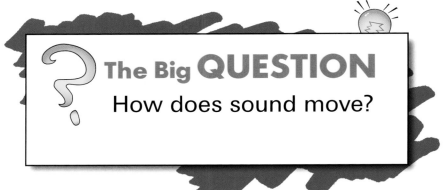

The Big QUESTION

How does sound move?

Sound Waves

When something vibrates, the air moves. It moves in waves. They are called **sound waves.** We cannot see sound waves. They move in all directions. They move through the air. They move like water waves.

Eardrum

Sound waves hit our ears. Sound waves move air inside our ears. The air makes our eardrums vibrate. The vibrations tell our brains what the sound is.

Sound Moves

Sound waves move through water. Animals can make sounds in water. Have you made sounds in water?

Dolphins make sounds in water.

Sound waves move through solid things. They can go through walls. They can move through doors.

CHECKPOINT

1. What are sound waves?

2. What can sound waves travel through?

 How does sound move?

ACTIVITY
How Sounds Travel

Find Out
Do this activity to hear how sound travels.

Process Skills
Observing
Communicating
Predicting

WHAT YOU NEED

bell

Activity Journal

WHAT TO DO

Ask your partner to ring the bell while you:

1. Stand in front of your partner and **listen.**

2. Stand behind your partner and **listen.**

3. Go to the back of the room and **listen** to the bell.

WHAT HAPPENED

1. What did you hear when you stood in front of your partner? Behind your partner?

2. **Tell** what you heard from the back of the room.

WHAT IF

Predict what you would hear if you went in the hallway and listened to the bell.

Review

What I Know

Choose the best word for each sentence.

music	soft	loud
vibrate	vibrations	high
low	sound waves	

1. A _____ sound is easier to hear than a soft sound.

2. You whisper to make a _____ sound.

3. Instruments can play _____.

4. A bee's wings _____ to make sound.

5. _____ make the air move.

6. Your throat vibrates slowly to make a _____ sound.

7. _____ can move through air, water, and solids.

1. Tell about the sounds in the picture.

2. Tell which sounds could be loud. Which could be soft?

3. Tell how the sounds would be different if you were on the street and if you were inside watching from a window.

For My Portfolio

Have a partner cover his or her eyes. Make a sound, and have your partner guess how you made it.

Unit Review

Telling About What I Learned

1. Matter can have three forms. Name them.

2. A magnet can push and pull. Name three things a magnet can attract.

3. Sound moves in waves called sound waves. Name two things that make sound.

Problem Solving

Use the picture to help answer the questions.

1. What kinds of sounds could this instrument make?

2. What makes the sounds?

Something to Do

Do a demonstration. Show how you can use a magnet to move things.

UNIT D

Health Science

YOUR BODY

People are all shapes and sizes. Have you ever noticed the way somebody walks? Nobody walks exactly the same way. But people are more alike than different.

The Big IDEA

People are more alike than different.

CHAPTER SCIENCE INVESTIGATION

Count your heartbeats. Find out what to do in your *Activity Journal.*

Bones, Muscles, and the Brain

Let's Find Out
- What your bones do
- What your muscles and brain do

Words to Know
bones
skeleton
muscles
brain

The Big QUESTION

Which body parts help you move and think?

Inside Your Body

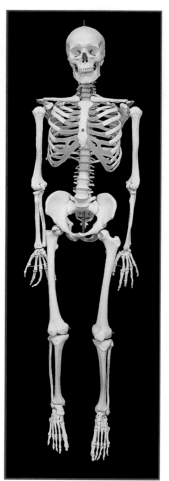

Your body has many parts. Each part has a job. Body parts work together. They help you do many things.

You can see and touch some body parts. But many parts are inside. You cannot see them. You cannot see your bones. **Bones** are inside your body.

You have many bones. They are different shapes and sizes. They help you stand and move. All the bones together are called the **skeleton.**

Doctors use machines to see inside your body. X rays are used to see your bones. What do you think these pictures show?

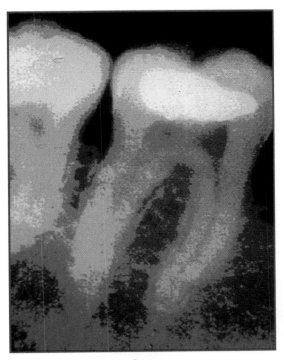

Tooth X ray

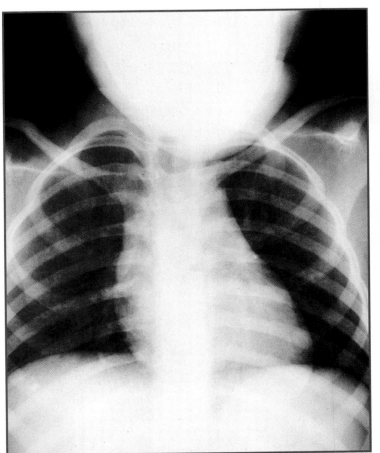

X ray

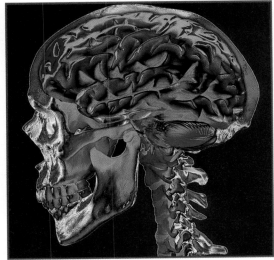

MRI

Your Muscles and Brain

Bones cannot move by themselves. **Muscles** move your bones. They help you walk, run, and kick a ball. Can you feel the muscles that move your leg?

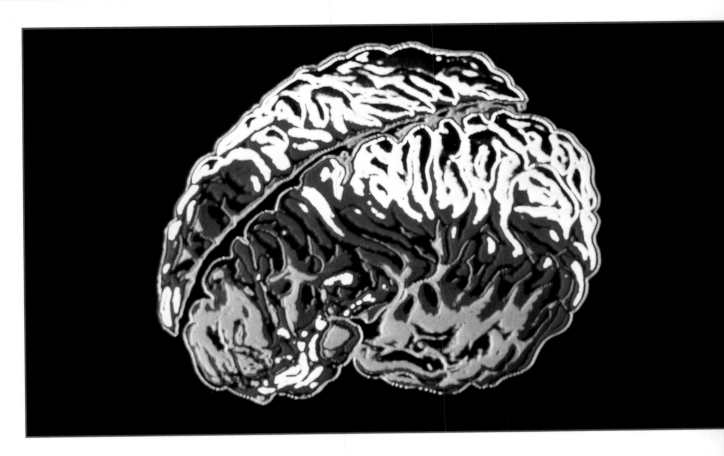

Your **brain** tells your body what to do. It helps you read, write, think, and move. Your brain is always working. It works even when you sleep.

CHECKPOINT

1. What do your bones do?

2. What do your muscles and brain do?

? Which body parts help you move and think?

ACTIVITY
Moving Muscles

Find Out
Do this activity to feel your muscles move.

Process Skills
Observing
Communicating
Predicting

WHAT YOU NEED

mirror

Activity Journal

WHAT TO DO

1. Hold your hand and arm out straight.
2. Put your other hand on the upper part of your arm.

3. Bend your arm at the elbow. **Feel** what happens to the muscles of your upper arm.

4. **Look** in a mirror. Make a funny face. **See** how many muscles you can move in your face.

WHAT HAPPENED

1. What did you feel when you bent your arm?

2. **Tell** how you knew your muscles were working in your arm and face.

WHAT IF

Predict what you would feel if you held a heavy book when you bent your arm.

The Heart, Lungs, and Stomach

Let's Find Out

- How blood moves
- What your lungs and stomach do

Words to Know

heart
blood
blood vessels
lungs
stomach

The Big QUESTION

What do your heart, lungs, and stomach do?

Blood Moves

Your **heart** is a muscle. It pumps **blood** to all parts of your body.

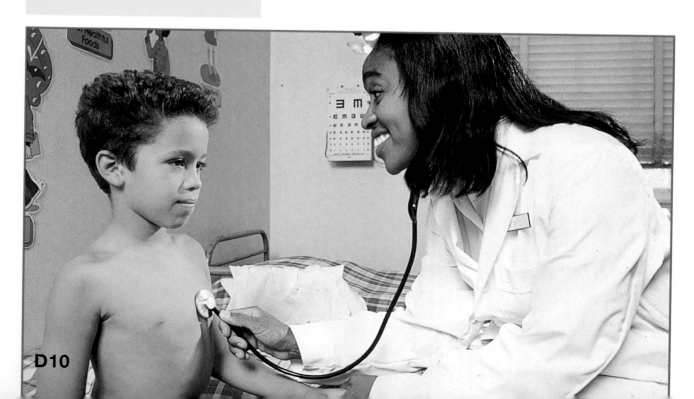

Blood moves through your body in tubes. These tubes are called **blood vessels.** Put your fingers on your neck. Can you feel your blood moving?

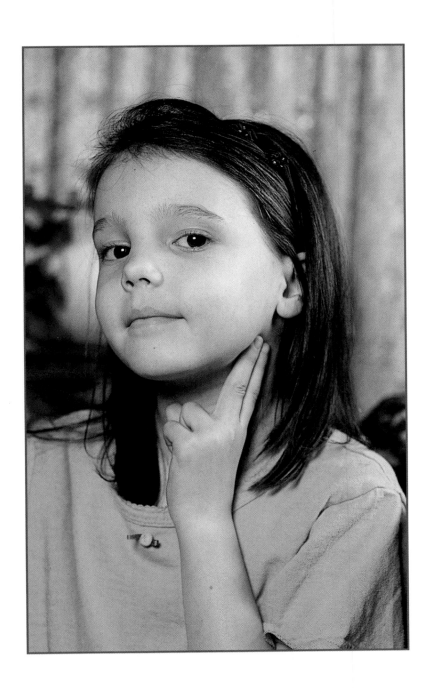

Your Lungs and Stomach

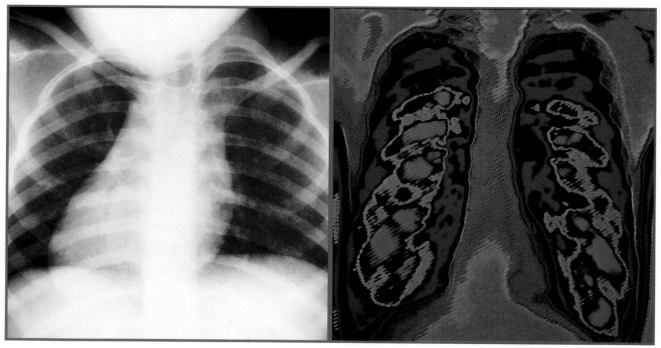

X ray   CAT scan

Take a deep breath. Your mouth and nose take in air. Air moves to your **lungs.** Your lungs help your body use air.

When you eat, your stomach stretches. Your **stomach** holds the food you eat. Your body uses some of the food. Some food leaves your body as waste.

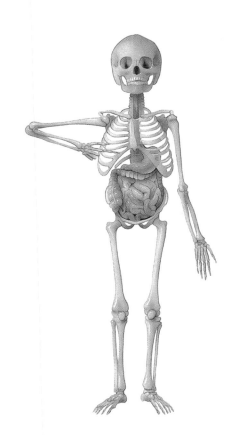

CHECKPOINT

1. How does blood move through your body?

2. What do your lungs and stomach do?

[?] What do your heart, lungs, and stomach do?

ACTIVITY

Watching Lung Power

Find Out
Do this activity to see how your lungs move.

Process Skills
Observing
Communicating
Constructing Models

WHAT YOU NEED

clear plastic bottle with lid

Activity Journal

goggles

balloon

WHAT TO DO

1. Hold the balloon by the end. Put the rest of the balloon in the bottle.

2. Stretch the opening of the balloon over the neck of the bottle.

3. Put the lid on the bottle. Open the spout.

4. **See** what happens to the balloon as you slowly squeeze the bottle.

WHAT HAPPENED

1. What happens to the balloon as you squeeze the bottle?

2. How is the balloon like your lungs?

WHAT IF

What would happen if you used a smaller balloon?

Each of You Is Different

Let's Find Out
- How people are alike
- How people are different

Words to Know
alike
different
fingerprint

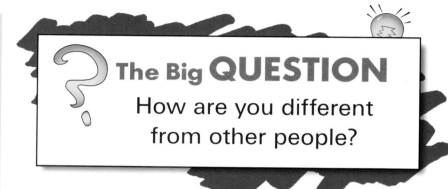

The Big QUESTION

How are you different from other people?

Alike

People are **alike** in many ways. People have bodies that work alike. Their bodies move, breathe, and use food.

All people have feelings.
People can be happy or sad.
They can be excited or scared.
People can even be mad.

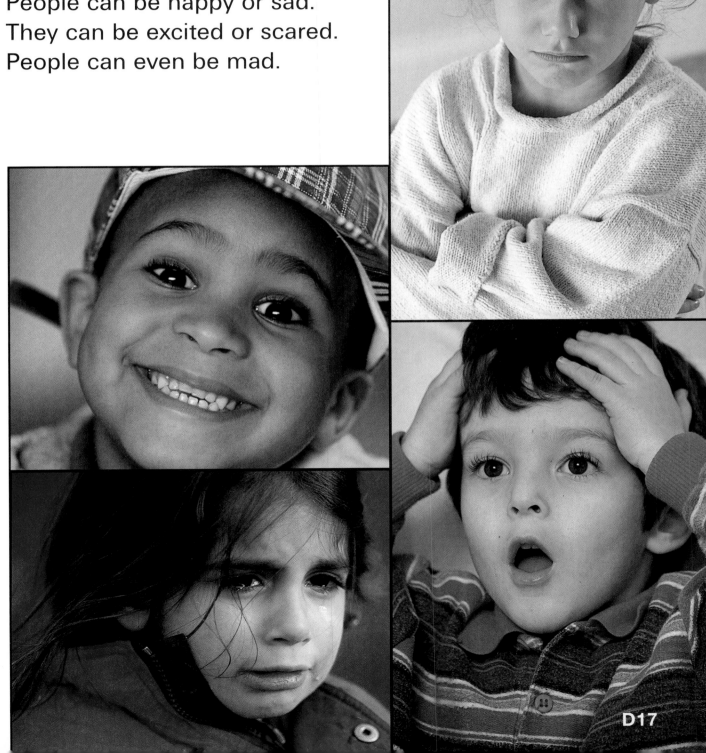

Different

People are **different** in some ways. No two people are exactly alike.

Look at the tiny lines on your fingertips. Everyone has a different **fingerprint.**

People like different activities. You may like to play soccer. Your friend may like to sing. Tell about some activities you like.

 CHECKPOINT

1. How are people alike?

2. How are people different?

[?] How are you different from other people?

ACTIVITY

Different Tastes

Find Out

Do this activity to see if people like the same kind of fruit.

Process Skills

Observing
Communicating
Using Numbers

WHAT YOU NEED

banana

apple

orange

paper plates

crayons

paper

scissors

chart paper

Activity Journal

WHAT TO DO

1. **Look** at the apple, orange, and banana slices on your plate.

2. **Draw** your favorite fruit. Cut it out.

   Safety! **Be careful with scissors.**

3. Make a class graph.

4. **Add** up the number of students who liked each fruit.

WHAT HAPPENED

1. How many students liked apples best? Oranges? Bananas?

2. What is the most popular fruit?

WHAT IF

If you tasted different kinds of juice, would everyone like the same one? Why or why not?

Review

What I Know

Choose the best word for each sentence.

brain	blood	bones
fingerprint	heart	skeleton
lungs	alike	muscles
blood vessels	stomach	different

1. Your _____ move your bones.

2. Your _____ pumps blood through your body.

3. Blood vessels move _____ through your body.

4. Your _____ help your body use air.

5. Your _____ holds the food you eat.

6. No two people are exactly _____.

7. Everyone's fingers make a different _____.

Using What I Know

1. How are these children alike?

2. How are these children different?

3. What activities do these children like to do?

For My Portfolio

Play charades. Without talking, move your body to show something that you like to do.

A Healthy Body

Your body is important for everything you do.

You need to care for your body. Taking care of your body helps you stay healthy and safe.

The Big IDEA

You can help yourself be healthy and safe.

Follow safety rules. Find out what to do in your *Activity Journal.*

Germs and Illness

Let's Find Out

- How germs can make you sick
- How you can help keep germs from spreading

Words to Know

germs

The Big QUESTION

How do germs spread?

Spreading Germs

Sometimes you might not feel well. Your head hurts. Your stomach aches. You might be sick.

Germs can make you sick. You cannot see them, but germs are everywhere.

Germs can enter your body in many ways. They can enter through your nose, eyes, or mouth. They can also enter through cuts in your skin.

Germs can spread from person to person. They can spread when you cough, sneeze, or shake someone's hand.

Keeping Clean

You can stop some germs from spreading. Wash your hands with soap and water. Cover your mouth when you cough. Do not share drinking glasses or silverware.

Keep objects out of your mouth. Keep your teeth clean. Brush and floss your teeth.

CHECKPOINT

1. How can germs make you sick?

2. How can you help keep germs from spreading?

 How do germs spread?

ACTIVITY

How Germs Spread

WHAT YOU NEED

water

baby oil

tape

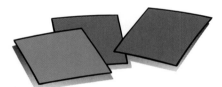
paper

newspaper

two spray bottles

Activity Journal

WHAT TO DO

1. Cover your work area with newspaper.

2. Tape two different-colored pieces of paper together.

3. Spray the water on one piece of paper. **Watch** what happens. **Safety!** **Do not spray toward other people.**

4. Spray the baby oil on the other piece of paper. **Watch** what happens. **Safety!** **Do not spray toward other people.**

WHAT HAPPENED

1. What happened when you sprayed the water? The baby oil?

2. How is sneezing like spraying the baby oil?

WHAT IF

What would happen if you covered the openings of the spray bottles?

Staying Well

Let's Find Out
- What medicine does
- What a vaccine is

Words to Know
medicine
vaccine

The Big QUESTION
How can you help to stay well?

Medicine

Think about the last time you were sick. How did you feel?

When you are sick, your body needs extra care.

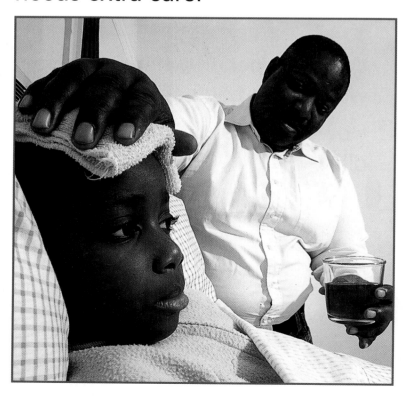

Sometimes you take medicine when you are sick. **Medicine** can change the way your body works. It can kill germs in your body. It can kill germs on your skin.

Only an adult should give you medicine.

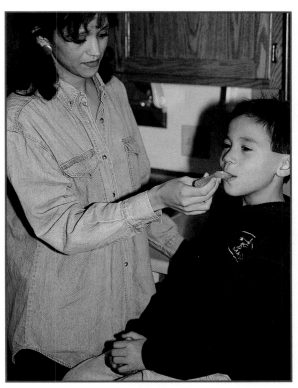

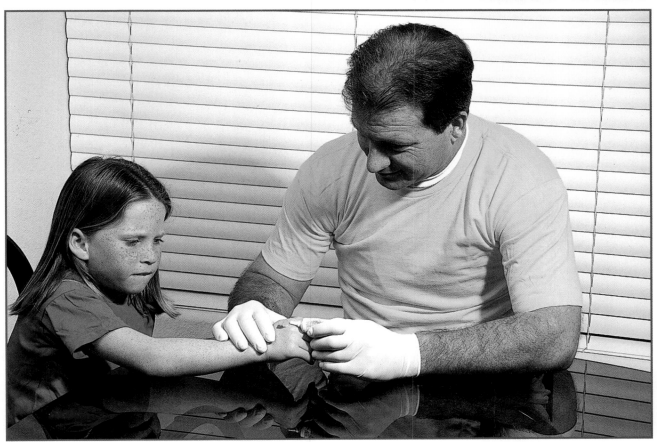

Vaccines

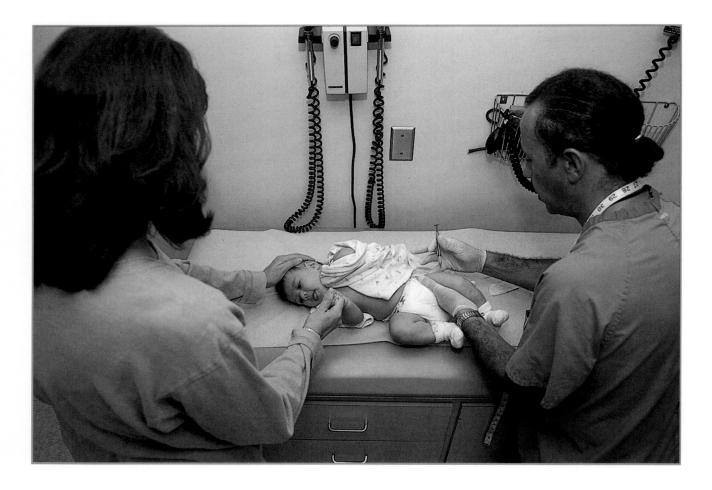

Some medicines can keep you from getting sick. A **vaccine** is a medicine that keeps your body safe from some germs.

Some vaccines are given in shots. Some go in your mouth.

A flu shot is one kind of vaccine. Have you had any vaccines?

CHECKPOINT

1. What does medicine do?

2. What is a vaccine?

How can you help to stay well?

ACTIVITY

Putting Medicine in Its Place

WHAT YOU NEED

Find Out
Do this activity to see where a safe place is to put medicine.

Process Skills
Communicating
Observing
Classifying

paper

magazines

crayons or markers

glue

scissors

Activity Journal

WHAT TO DO

1. Use your paper as a medicine cabinet. **Draw** what your cabinet looks like.

2. **Look** for pictures of medicines in the magazines. Cut them out. **Safety!** **Be careful with scissors.**

3. Can you put these medicines in **groups?** How?

4. Glue them on your cabinet.

WHAT HAPPENED

1. **Tell** what medicines you found.

2. Who should give you medicine?

WHAT IF

If you find some medicine at home, what should you do with it?

• LESSON 3

Safety

Let's Find Out
- What you can do at school to be safe
- What you can do at home to be safe

Words to Know
safety rules
accident

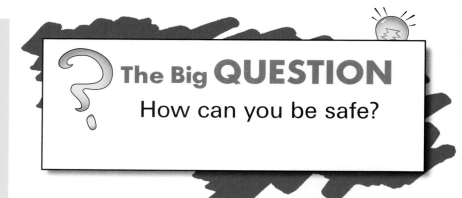

The Big QUESTION
How can you be safe?

Rules at School

To stay healthy, you need to be safe. Following **safety rules** helps keep you safe.

You can be safe going to and from school. Wait for the school bus on the curb. Never walk in front of the bus, behind the bus, or too close to the bus. Always talk softly on the bus. The driver needs to hear at all times. Keep hands, arms, and head inside the bus.

You can be safe in your classroom. Always walk. Do not run. Keep legs of chairs on the floor. Be careful with scissors.

What are some other safety rules you have in your classroom?

Rules at Home

You can be safe at home. If you are not safe, you might have an **accident.** An accident can cause you harm.

Be careful in the kitchen. Always ask an adult for help in the kitchen. Some things might be hot or sharp.

Be careful when you are playing. Always wear a helmet when you are riding your bike or skating.

Never play with matches. If there is a fire, get out as fast as you can. Then call for help. Plan a spot for everyone in your family to meet. Listen to the firefighters. If your clothes catch on fire, stop, drop, and roll.

CHECKPOINT

1. Name a safety rule at school.

2. Name a safety rule at home.

 How can you be safe?

ACTIVITY
Preventing Accidents

Find Out

Do this activity to see how people follow rules.

Process Skills

Observing

Communicating

WHAT YOU NEED

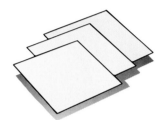
poster paper

magazines

marker

glue

scissors

Activity Journal

ruler

WHAT TO DO

1. Use your ruler to divide the poster paper into two parts.

2. Label one half of the paper "At School." Label the other half "At Home."

3. **Look** for pictures in the magazines showing people being safe.

4. Glue the pictures to the correct part of the poster.

WHAT HAPPENED

1. **Tell** about the pictures you cut out.

2. **Tell** how you stay safe like someone on your poster.

WHAT IF

What other place could you make safety rules for?

Review

What I Know

Choose the best word for each sentence.

accident	**germs**	**vaccine**
medicine	**safety rules**	

1. Sneezing spreads _____.

2. If you are sick, a doctor might give you _____.

3. A _____ is medicine that keeps your body safe from some germs.

4. Following _____ can help keep you safe.

5. If you are not careful, you might have an _____.

Using What I Know

Use the picture to answer the questions.

1. What are the bicycle riders wearing to stay safe?

2. How does this help them stay safe?

3. Tell another time when wearing a helmet is a good safety rule to follow.

4. Name one more safety rule a bicycle rider should know.

5. Name one more way to stay safe outside.

For My **Portfolio**

Pretend you are a police officer.
What safety rules would you look for?

Feeding Your

Your body can do many things.
It needs food to do work. You
need food to bike, swim, and play.

The Big IDEA

You need food to
grow strong
and healthy.

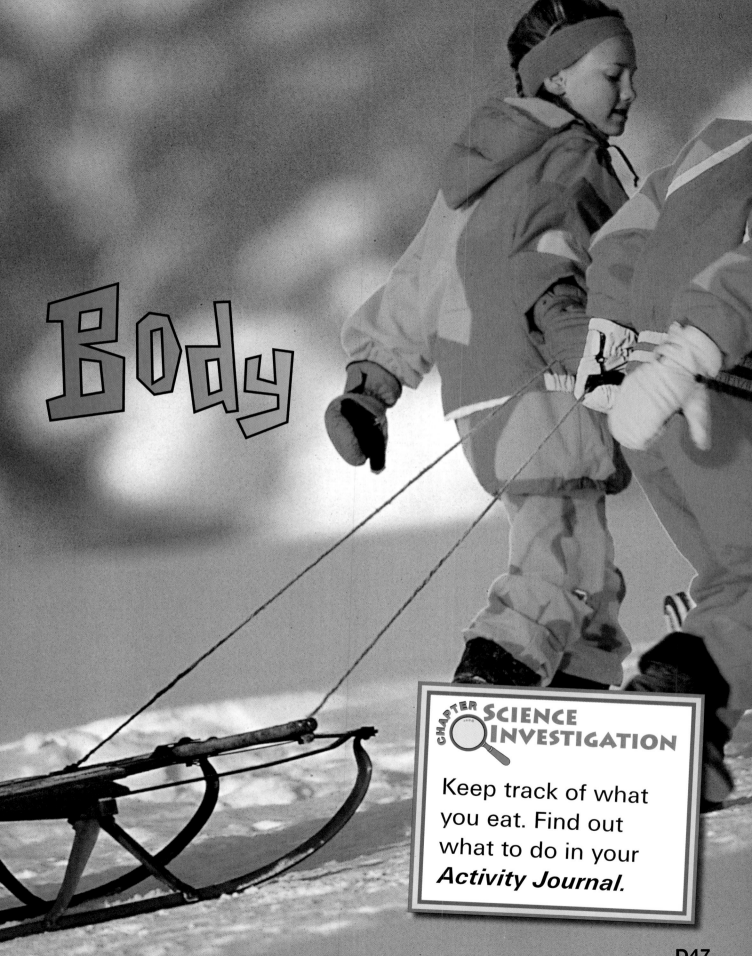

Body

CHAPTER SCIENCE INVESTIGATION

Keep track of what you eat. Find out what to do in your *Activity Journal.*

Food Groups

Let's Find Out

- What foods come from plants
- What foods come from animals

Words to Know

fruits
vegetables
grains
milk
sweets

The Big QUESTION

What kinds of foods are there?

Food from Plants

Many healthful foods are from plants.

Fruits and **vegetables** come from plants. Pineapples and bananas are fruits. Snow peas and carrots are vegetables. There are many different kinds of fruits and vegetables.

Beans and nuts come from plants.

Grains come from plants, too. Bread, rice, and cereal are grains. Tortillas and noodles are made from grains.

Food from Animals

Some food comes from animals. **Milk** comes from mammals like cows and goats. Cheese, yogurt, and ice cream are made with milk.

Meat and chicken come from animals. Fish and eggs come from animals, too.

Most foods are good for you.
Some foods are not. **Sweets** like
candy and cookies have sugar.
Too much sugar is not good for
your teeth.

CHECKPOINT

1. Name three foods from plants.

2. Name three foods from animals.

 What kinds of foods are there?

ACTIVITY

Grouping Foods

Find Out

Do this activity to see where some foods come from.

Process Skills

Observing
Classifying
Communicating

paper

glue

scissors

magazines

Activity Journal

WHAT TO DO

1. Fold your paper to make two parts. Write "Food from Plants" on one part. Write "Food from Animals" on the other part.

2. **Look** at the magazines. Find pictures of food. Cut them out.
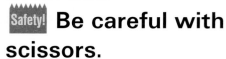 **Be careful with scissors.**

3. Make **groups** of food from plants and groups of food from animals.

4. Glue the pictures where they belong.

WHAT HAPPENED

1. **Tell** what foods you put in each group.

2. Could you put some foods in both groups? If so, which ones?

WHAT IF

Name one thing you ate today. Tell whether it came from plants or animals or both.

All Kinds of Food

Let's Find Out

- What kinds of food help your body stay healthy
- How food can help you stay strong
- How you get energy from food

Words to Know

energy
fuel

The Big QUESTION

How do different foods help your body?

Staying Healthy

Healthful food helps your body. Each kind of healthful food helps your body in a different way.

Grains give you **energy.** You need energy to run, play, and grow. You need energy to think and read.

You should eat at least six servings of grains each day.

Fruits and vegetables help your body. Carrots help your eyes. Oranges help your skin.

You need three to five servings of vegetables each day. You need two to four servings of fruit.

Staying Strong

Foods made from milk have calcium. Calcium helps you grow. It helps your bones and teeth be strong. Name some foods that have calcium.

You need two to three servings from the milk group each day.

Some foods build strong muscles. Meat from cows and chickens helps your muscles. Beans and nuts do, too. Tell what other foods help your muscles.

You need two or three servings from the meat group every day.

Fuel for Your Body

Your body has many parts. All the parts work together so you can move and grow.

Your body needs food from all of the groups to keep it working. Food is **fuel** for your body. Fuel gives you energy.

Eating healthful meals gives you energy.

Sometimes you use up your energy. Eating a snack can help. Fruits and vegetables are healthful snacks. Tell what healthful snacks you like.

CHECKPOINT

1. What kinds of food help your body stay healthy?

2. How can food help you stay strong?

3. How do you get energy from food?

 How do different foods help your body?

ACTIVITY

Choosing Healthful Food

Find Out
Do this activity to plan a healthful meal.

Process Skills
Classifying
Communicating

WHAT YOU NEED

 magazines

 glue

 scissors

 paper plate

 *Activity Journal*

WHAT TO DO

1. Find pictures of healthful food in magazines.

2. Cut out the pictures. Put them in **groups.**
   Safety! Be careful with scissors.

3. Plan a healthful meal. Choose food pictures from each **group.**

4. Glue the pictures you choose on your plate.

WHAT HAPPENED

1. What foods did you pick?

2. **Tell** how each food helps your body.

WHAT IF

Plan a healthful meal for your family. What foods would you choose?

Where Food Comes From

Let's Find Out
- What foods come from farms
- How foods get from the farm to the grocery store

Words to Know
grocery store
farms
farmers

 **The Big QUESTION**
Where does the food you eat come from?

Food from Farms

You can see all kinds of food at a **grocery store.** Where does all that food come from?

Many of the foods you eat are grown on **farms.**

Farmers grow grains, fruits, and vegetables.

Some farmers raise animals. Meat, eggs, and milk come from animals. Tell what foods come from these animals.

From Farm to Grocery Store

Farmers gather all of their food. Some goes to a factory. The factory cooks some food. Then they put it in packages.

Other food from the farm goes straight to the store. Trucks, trains, boats, and planes carry food from farms to stores.

CHECKPOINT

1. What foods do farmers grow?

2. How does food get to the grocery store?

? Where does the food you eat come from?

ACTIVITY

Grouping Food from Farms

Find Out
Do this activity to see what foods come from a farm.

Process Skills
Observing
Communicating
Classifying

WHAT YOU NEED

cup

Activity Journal

two plates

variety of foods

WHAT TO DO

1. **Look** at your food.
2. **Tell** about each one.

3. Put your food in **groups. Tell** how you put them in **groups.**

4. Put your food in different **groups. Tell** what you did.

WHAT HAPPENED

1. **Tell** the different ways you put your food in **groups.**

2. What foods went to a factory to be made?

WHAT IF

Tell about a hamburger. Where do all of the parts of it come from? How does it get to your plate?

Review

What I Know

Choose the best word for each sentence.

sweets	energy	fruits
vegetables	farmers	farms
milk	grocery store	fuel
grains		

1. Apples and bananas are _____.

2. Rice, bread, and cereal are _____.

3. _____ helps your bones and teeth stay strong.

4. _____ have a lot of sugar.

5. Grains give you _____.

6. You buy food at the _____.

7. Food is grown on _____.

Using What I Know

1. Tell what kinds of food you see in this picture.

2. Which foods come from plants? Which come from animals?

3. Which foods do you need to stay healthy?

For My Portfolio

Describe your favorite food. Tell what it looks and tastes like. Have a partner guess what food it is. Then tell what plants and animals it is made from. Tell how it keeps you healthy.

Unit Review

Telling About What I Learned

1. People are more alike than different. How are people alike?

2. You can keep yourself healthy and safe. Name two things you can do to stay safe.

3. You need food to grow strong and healthy. Name four kinds of food you need.

Problem Solving

Use the picture to answer the questions.

1. Tell what foods you see.

2. How does each food help you?

Something to Do

Think about three body parts.

Create a dance using all three.

Reference

Almanac

Animal Bodies

Giraffe

Skeleton	Body Covering	Animal

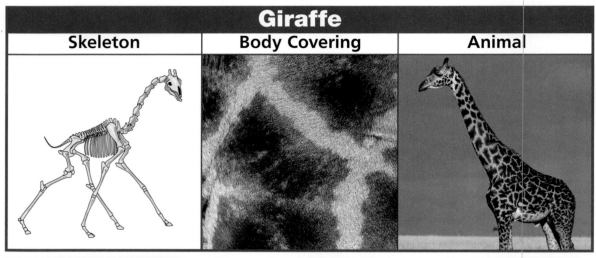

Elephant

Skeleton	Body Covering	Animal

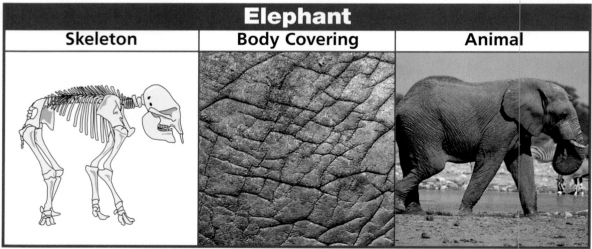

Owl

Skeleton	Body Covering	Animal

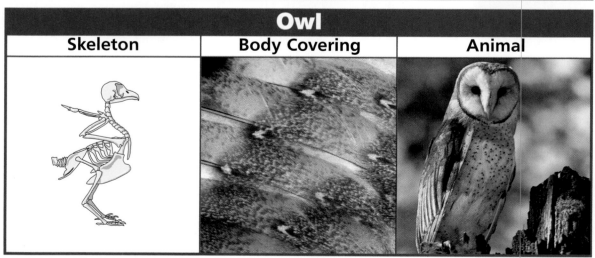

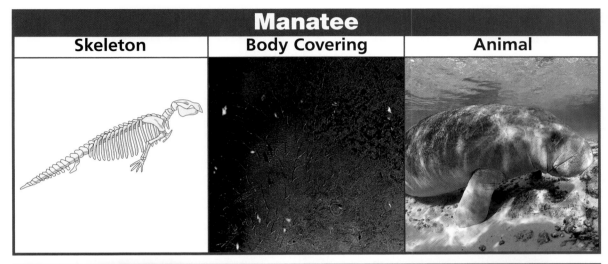

Manatee

Skeleton	Body Covering	Animal

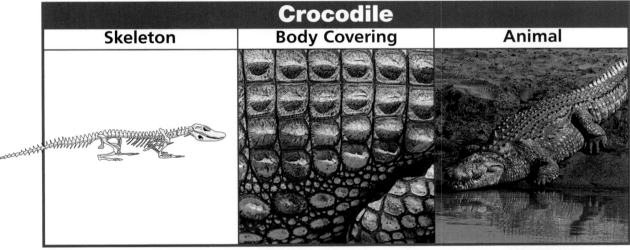

Crocodile

Skeleton	Body Covering	Animal

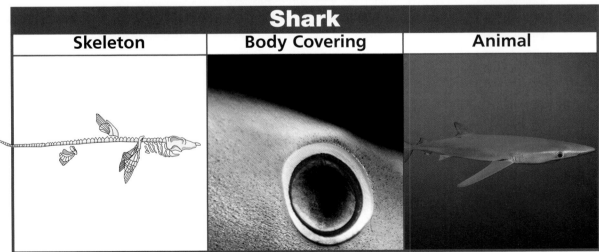

Shark

Skeleton	Body Covering	Animal

United States

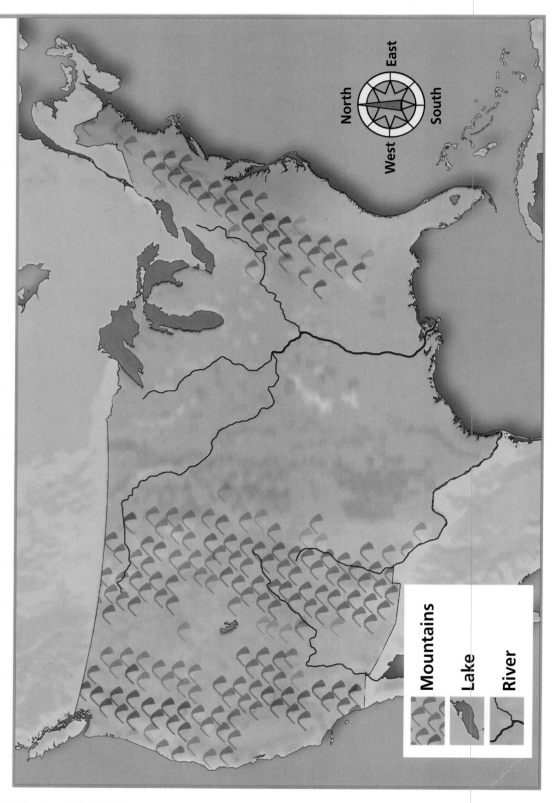

North
East
South
West

Mountains

Lake

River

Minerals

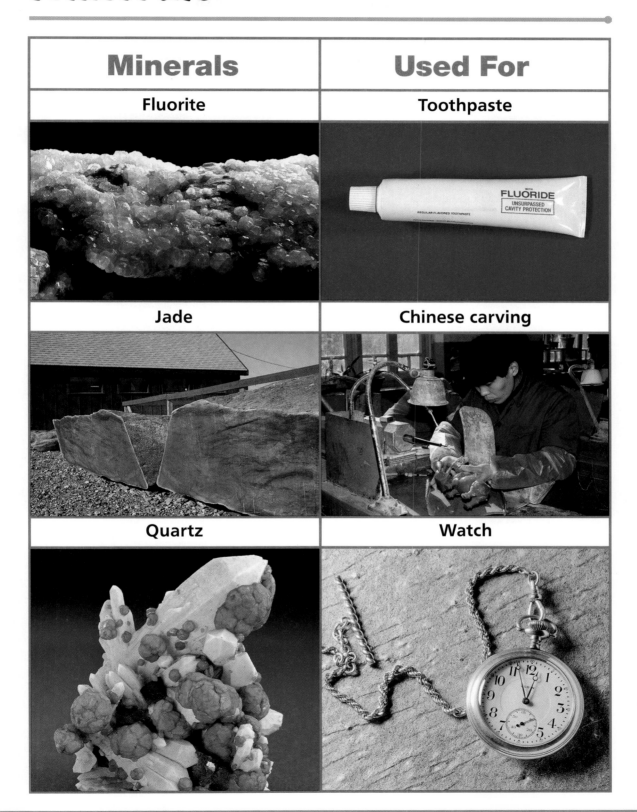

Minerals	Used For
Fluorite	Toothpaste
Jade	Chinese carving
Quartz	Watch

Forms of Matter

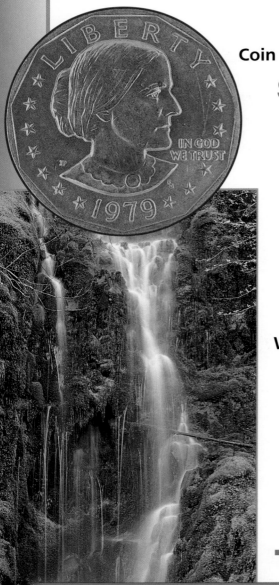

Coin

Solids

Helmet

Water

Liquids

Honey

Things with Gases

Balloon

Blimp

What Makes the Sound?

Air Vibrates

Flute

Trombone

Strings Vibrate

Harp

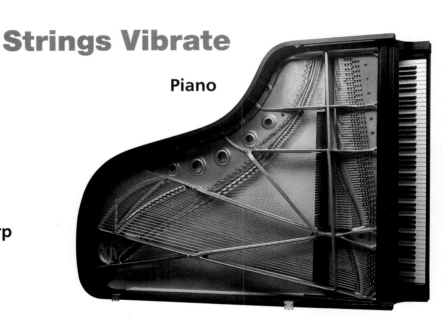

Piano

Hit or Shake

Cymbals

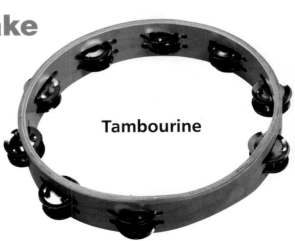

Tambourine

Your Body

Outside Your Body

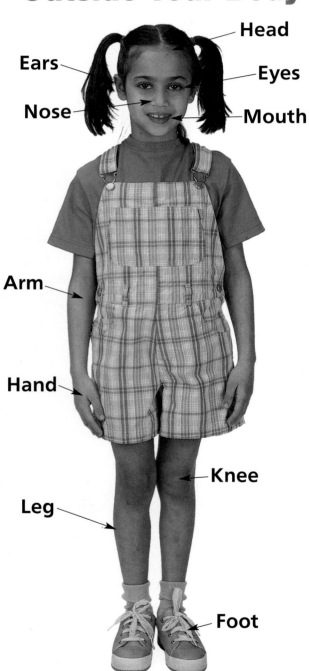

Head

Ears

Eyes

Nose

Mouth

Arm

Hand

Knee

Leg

Foot

Inside Your Body

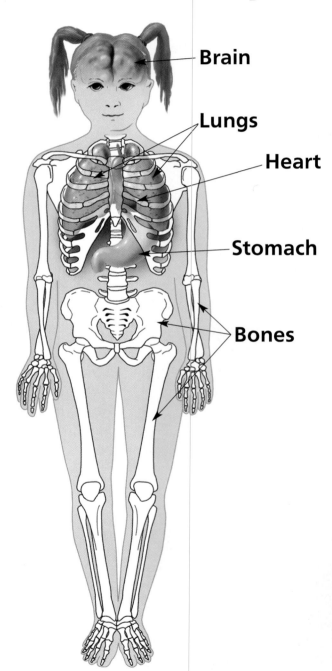

Brain

Lungs

Heart

Stomach

Bones

Fruits and Seeds

Orange

Watermelon

Apples

Glossary

A

accident, page D40

If you are not careful, you might have an **accident.**

air, pages A4, B5, and B63

Animals and plants need **air** to live.

alike, page D16

Things that look **alike** look the same.

amphibians, page A30

Frogs and toads are **amphibians.**

Arctic, page B38

It can be very cold in the **Arctic.**

attract, page C33

Magnets **attract** some metals.

B

beaks, page A7

Birds use their **beaks** to help them eat.

birds, page A27

Birds fly through the air.

Glossary

blood, page D10

Your heart pumps **blood** through your body.

blood vessels, page D11

Blood vessels carry your blood in your body.

bones, page D4

Your **bones** are inside your body.

brain, page D7

Your **brain** helps you think.

c

cactus, page A58

A **cactus** lives in a desert.

cattails, page A65

Cattails grow in swamps.

climate, page B26

The **climate** of a desert is dry.

cold, page B38

The Arctic is a **cold** place.

cones, page A43

Pine trees keep their seeds inside **cones**.

Glossary

D

desert, pages A56 and B27

It rains very little in a **desert.**

different, page D18

All people are **different** from one another.

dry, page B27

When there is no rain, the land may be **dry.**

E

Earth, page B4

There is land and water on **Earth.**

eggs, page A35

Birds lay **eggs** in their nests.

egrets, page A63

Many **egrets** live in swamps.

energy, page D54

Food can give you **energy.**

Glossary

F

fall, page B18

Fall is a cooler season than summer.

farmers, page D63

Farmers grow many crops.

farms, page D62

Food is grown on **farms.**

feathers, page A27

Birds have some **feathers** that help them fly.

fingerprint, page D18

A finger can make a **fingerprint.**

fish, page A28

Fish swim in water.

flowers, page A11

Some plants have **flowers**.

food, page A4

Animals need **food** to live.

Glossary

freshwater, page B50

Rivers and lakes have **freshwater.**

fruits, pages A42 and D48

Bananas and apples are **fruits.**

fuel, page D58

Your body gets **fuel** from food.

fur, page A26

A bear has thick **fur** in winter.

G

gas, page C7

Air is a **gas** that you cannot see.

germs, page D26

Germs can make you sick.

grains, page D49

Bread and rice are **grains.**

Glossary

grocery store, page D62

Many people buy food at a **grocery store**.

H

habitat, page A16

An animal lives in a **habitat**.

heart, page D10

Your **heart** is a muscle that pumps blood.

heat, page C10

Heat makes things feel warmer.

high, page C57

Your throat vibrates fast to make a **high** sound.

hot, page B28

The air in a desert can get very **hot**.

humid, page B35

Humid air feels sticky.

I

ice, page B38

If it is very cold, water becomes **ice**.

Glossary

insects, page A31

Ladybugs are **insects**.

L

land, page B62

Bears live on **land**.

landforms, page B48

Plains and mountains are **landforms**.

leaves, page A11

Green **leaves** help plants make food.

liquid, page C6

Apple juice is a **liquid**.

loud, page C49

Fireworks make a **loud** sound.

low, page C57

When you make a **low** sound, your throat vibrates slowly.

lungs, page D12

Your **lungs** help you breathe.

Glossary

M

machines, page C39

Machines help you do work.

magnets, page C32

Magnets attract some metals.

mammals, page A26

Mammals have hair on their bodies.

matter, page C4

Matter can be a solid, liquid, or gas.

meadow, page A16

Some bees and snakes live in a meadow.

medicine, page D33

You may need medicine when you are sick.

melt, page C12

Ice will melt if it gets warm.

Glossary

milk, page D50

Cows and goats make **milk.**

minerals, page B55

Rocks are made of many **minerals.**

mixture, page C16

A **mixture** has two or more things in it.

muscles, page D6

Your leg **muscles** move your leg.

music, page C50

You can play **music** with an instrument.

N

nests, page A47

Birds build **nests** to live in.

Glossary

O

ocean, page A18

Many fish and coral live in an **ocean.**

P

pollen, page A49

Flowers have **pollen** to help make seeds.

predict, page B13

You can look at the sky and **predict** the weather.

pull, page C26

When you get into a car, you **pull** the door closed.

push, page C26

When you get out of a car, you **push** the door closed.

R

rain gauge, page B12

A **rain gauge** shows how much rain fell.

ramp, page C39

A **ramp** is a machine that helps you move things.

recycle, page B65

You can **recycle** cans, glass, and paper.

Glossary

repel, page C34

When magnets push each other, they **repel.**

reptiles, page A29

Snakes and lizards are **reptiles.**

resources, page B63

Land, water, and air are Earth's **resources.**

rocks, page B54

Mountains are made of many **rocks.**

roots, page A11

Roots take in water and nutrients from soil.

S

safety rules, page D38

Safety rules are rules that help you be safe.

salt water, page B50

The water in oceans is **salt water.**

Glossary

sand, page B58

Rocks can break down into small pieces called **sand.**

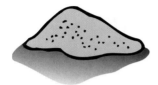

scales, page A28

Fish and reptiles have **scales** to keep them safe.

season, page B16

Summer is the warmest **season.**

seeds, page A13

Seeds can grow into new plants.

skeleton, page D5

All your bones make up your **skeleton.**

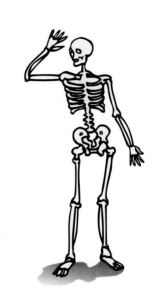

soft, page C49

A **soft** sound is hard to hear.

soil, page B59

Plants grow in **soil.**

Glossary

solid, page C5

A **solid** has a certain shape.

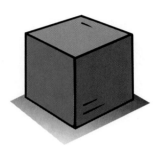

sound waves, page C62

Sound waves move in all directions.

speed, page C28

The **speed** of an object is how fast or slow it goes.

spring, page B17

Many plants begin to grow and bloom in **spring.**

stems, page A11

Stems carry water from the roots to the leaves.

stomach, page D13

After you eat food, it moves to your **stomach.**

summer, page B18

Summer comes after spring.

Glossary

sun, page B4

The **sun** can make the land and water warm.

swamps, page A62

Alligators and egrets live in **swamps.**

sweets, page D51

Candy and cookies are **sweets.**

T

tadpoles, page A37

When frogs are young, they are called **tadpoles.**

teeth, page A6

Animals use **teeth** to eat.

temperature, page B11

The **temperature** tells how warm or cool something is.

thermometer, page B11

You can use a **thermometer** to tell about the air.

Glossary

tropical rain forest, page B32

It rains a lot in a **tropical rain forest**.

V

vaccine, page D34

You can take a **vaccine** to keep from getting sick.

vegetables, page D48

Broccoli and carrots are **vegetables**.

vibrate, page C54

To **vibrate** is to move back and forth.

vibrations, page C54

Vibrations can make sounds.

W

water, pages A4 and B63

Animals drink **water**. They need **water** to live.

weather, page B5

You can feel the air to tell about the **weather**.

wet, page B33

Tropical rain forests and swamps are **wet**.

Glossary

wind, page B5

Air that moves is called **wind.**

wind sock, page B12

A **wind sock** shows which way the wind is moving.

winter, page B17

In some places, it snows in **winter.**

Index

A

accident, D40–D43

Activities

Big Push, Little Push, C30–C31

Building a Beak, A8–A9

Building Animal Models, A32–A33

Building Nests, A50–A51

Caring for Earth, B66–B67

Changing Water, C14–C15

Choosing Healthful Food, D60–D61

Comparing Eggs, A38–A39

Different Tastes, D20–D21

Freezing Earth, B42–B43

Gas Takes Up Space, C8–C9

Grouping Food from Farms, D66–D67

Grouping Foods, D52–D53

Grouping Rocks, B60–B61

Growing Seeds, A44–A45

Hearing Sounds, C52–C53

Hot and Dry, B30–B31

How Germs Spread, D30–D31

How Plants Get Water, A14–A15

How Sounds Travel, C66–C67

Making a Desert Diorama, A60–A61

Making a Land and Water Collage, B52–B53

Making a Season Wheel, B20–B21

Making a Swamp Mural, A66–A67

Making Different Sounds, C60–C61

Making Mixtures, C20–C21

Moving Muscles, D8–D9

Index

Index

Index

Index

Index

Credits